OUT OF THE TURRET

AND INTO HELL

Earl Benson
M/Sgt. USAF. RET.

OUT OF THE TURRET
AND
INTO HELL

V. Elaine Benson

OUT OF THE TURRET
AND
INTO HELL

V. Elaine Benson

Book layout and cover by V. Elaine Benson. Editing by V. E. Benson with special thanks to assistant editor, K. M. Wieland.

Mail orders will be filled upon receipt of check or money order.
$25.00 includes postage and handling, (American) payable to V.E. Benson.
Send to:

V. Elaine Benson
1317 N. Matlock Street
Mesa, AZ. 85203-4324

National Library of Canada Cataloguing in Publication Data

Benson, V. Elaine, 1951-
  Out of the turret and into hell
  "Life of a prisoner of war".
  Includes bibliographical references.
  ISBN 1-55212-852-0
  I. Title.
PS3602.E676O97 2001   813'.6   C2001-911041-3

TRAFFORD

This book was published *on-demand* in cooperation with Trafford Publishing.
On-demand publishing is a unique process and service of making a book available for retail sale to the public taking advantage of on-demand manufacturing and Internet marketing.
On-demand publishing includes promotions, retail sales, manufacturing, order fulfilment, accounting and collecting royalties on behalf of the author.

Suite 6E, 2333 Government St., Victoria, B.C. V8T 4P4, CANADA
Phone   250-383-6864   Toll-free   1-888-232-4444 (Canada & US)
Fax   250-383-6804   E-mail   sales@trafford.com
Web site   www.trafford.com   TRAFFORD PUBLISHING IS A DIVISION OF TRAFFORD HOLDINGS LTD.
Trafford Catalogue #01-0252   www.trafford.com/robots/01-0252.html

10   9   8   7   6   5   4   3

OUT OF THE TURRET AND INTO HELL

This autobiographical work of fiction, brings forth the experiences of a man who touched many lives, and was first done to preserve history for future generations, the format based on interviews, notes, and memory. It is called fiction only because of the author's wonderful re-creation of scenes and conversations. Everything herein is.... his true life.

Life in 1930s - 1940s America was not easy. The Great Depression and World War II affected how people lived, and survived. As you travel through the account of this WWII gunner's memories, it's hoped you'll experience an exciting, eye-opening adventure. It is also hoped.... that some will be inspired and gain insight as to how circumstances can shape a person into a survivor. It is my desire.... that some shall learn why freedom should never be taken for granted.

-V. Elaine Benson

To the memory of
those
who were there.

To
Earl,
who lived it.

TABLE OF CONTENTS

INTRODUCTION - OUT OF THE TURRET AND INTO HELL

OUT OF THE TURRET AND INTO HELL

In the spring of 1931, a Connecticut orphanage opened huge mouth like doors. Five frightened brothers were swept into dank grayness, swallowed up like unwanted puppies dropped off at a pound.

Nine-year-old Earl Benson sensed this as he and his brothers were assigned beds and told where to put belongings.

I'm the reason we're here. The dream says I'm bad, doesn't it? Why won't it go away? Why is God punishing me?

He couldn't remember when the dream had first appeared, but it was long ago, and always the same formidable nightmare. It would take a dozen years and a major global conflict to shed meaning on the frightening vision with its oppressive aspects.

CHAPTER ONE

SOAP IS CHEAP

Five-year-old Earl Benson let out a whoop as he raced his brothers to the driveway on a warm Saturday afternoon in September of 1927. Older brothers, Kenneth, Howard, and Edward, who preferred to be called Red, piled into the family's four-door sedan, followed by Earl and younger brothers, Johnny and Ernie. Their father backed the car out, then drove up Webster Street. Everyone waved at Mrs. McKissick and Mrs. Yabrosky, who sat on McKissicks' porch swing, catching up on neighborhood gossip.

"There go the Bensons," said Mrs. McKissick.

"Yup. Can't miss the bunch, all of them so fair-skinned and topped with that strawberry blonde hair, and those crystal-blue eyes! Sure's a shame Hazel lost her twins last year. Boy and a girl.... What'd she call them?"

"Charles and Charlette. Having her twelfth any day now. She was married before, you know. Figure she was about seventeen. Said his name was George, something. Her oldest two were born in New York State. Don't know what happened, she's never said much, but here she is, married to this dear, sweet, God-fearing man, and look at his patience!"

"Lord, yes, and such a hard worker, fixing the old Polish dance hall into a nice home and putting in all those hours at the mill. Why, Unionville could use more gentlemen like him."

Earl loved rides. Dad was going to the market to make a payment. Ma usually paid, leaving the boys home with their sisters, but wasn't feeling well. Today was special, as the grocer gave the boys penny candy when Pa paid. John Henry smiled and pulled nickels from his ears, one coin for each son.

Taking his, Earl said, "Thanks, Pa," then rushed to the candy counter for a handful of treats.

While John Henry conducted business, the boys waited outside. Each checked their purchase, compared it with brothers', deals were made, and candy traded, until their father came out.

Sweets tucked away, they piled into the car. Cheeks bulging like chipmunks' returning from an acorn feast, the five brothers laughed and poked each other until colorful drool made its way down sticky chins. Salivations were caught by fingers and sucked into mouths, then the fingers were licked clean.

John Henry hollered, loud enough to be heard, "Don't mess the upholstery!" But it was so good and special that hardly a drop or delectable morsel got away.

BENSON HOME - 72 WEBSTER ST, UNIONVILLE, CONNECTICUT

2

Saturday nights meant hustle and bustle in the Bensons' warm kitchen. Baths were taken in tin tubs in the middle of the floor. Pots of water heated on a cookstove that stood in one corner. One end of the room held a table with long benches to seat the children. High-backed chairs stood at each end for the grownups.

Ma delegated, as daughters helped younger brothers tug off clothes, and older brothers kept things orderly. Towels, washclothes, and nightclothes were stacked along one bench.

Two-and-a-half-year-old Ernie stood under the table, wailing, "No baff!" as ten-year-old Alice tried to undress him. Mister Benson entered, snatched a potholder and, whistling softly, checked and stirred a pot of maple syrup boiling on the back of the stove. Long hours as a spinner at Myrtle Knitting Mill in Unionville left little time to do much but discipline his children, which he did with fair, sometimes good-humored, consistency. Kneeling, he looked into Ernie's eyes.

"Come here, Son." Ernie's wails ended. He ran to Pa, who said, "Alice is giving you a bath, so I want you to be a big boy." Tousle-haired Ernie, face tear streaked and grimy, wiped his nose on his sleeve. He loved talking with his father.

"Baff hurt?" John Henry laughed.

"No, Son, baths do not hurt. Alice will let you wash your own face tonight if you don't fuss. Okay?" Ernie grinned.

"Kay! I weddy, Ahwiss!" Then, it was Earl's turn.

"Why do we got to take baths and have clean clothes all the time?" Ma's voice was shrill.

"Cleanliness is next to godliness! You don't have to be rich to be clean. Soap is cheap, and just 'cause your clothes ain't new, doesn't mean they can't be clean!" Earl closed his mouth and got into the tub. When Ma spoke, all listened. She ran a clean home, kept a tight hand on money, taught politeness,

3

respect, manners, and demanded the best behavior of her children in school, church, at home, and in public.

November 6, 1927, baby Bernard, was born. Thirteen-year-old Shirley, twelve-year-old Edith, and Alice were kept busy with chores and tending their younger brothers. Everyone worked. Money earned, including Mister Benson's, was turned over to Mrs. Benson. From the whole amount, she gave them a small allowance.

February, 1928, baby Bernard died. Earl didn't know why Ma was different. She looked sad as she kept things going smoothly. She was a good cook, able to turn a pound of hamburger into a large gourmet meal by making meatloaf for her hungry bunch. Sometimes they had fried porkchops, five or six, if afforded. Vegetables were cheap, the garden helped, the children gathered nuts and berries and, often, the older brothers brought home meat from hunting, trapping, or fishing.

At mealtime, they waited until Pa was served. He took what he wanted, usually not much, then Ma handed the platter to the ones responsible for nabbing the meat. She took a small piece and, if any was left, she divided it into small portions for the rest. Sometimes, a sibling didn't want any, and it was great when Earl was told he could have the last piece.

"Excuse me." Earl, two front teeth gone, looked at his father who sat at the head of the table. "Dad, when can I learn to soot the gun, so I can get a squirrel for supper?" He smiled.

Calling Pa Dad just might do the trick. Pa studied him, blue eyes twinkling as they peered over wire-rimmed spectacles.

"How old are you, Son?"

"Six, but I'll be seven pretty soon!" Mister Benson took a bite, then chewed thoughtfully. Earl wiggled his fingers around his biscuit.

"There's another year or so, at least, before you touch the

4

BB gun, let alone the twenty-two." Earl frowned and was trying to decide how much longer that would be when Red nudged him hard in the ribs.

"I don't get to touch 'em yet, so why d'you think you should?" Earl glared at his older brother. Well-ordered conversations were allowed at the table as long as no one interrupted and everyone's conduct was proper and polite. God help a child who reached in front of someone for another helping or got caught chewing, mouth open, because, like as not, he'd be rapped on the knuckles with whichever utensil Ma happened to be using. She nailed Red with a fork and he let out a yelp.

"You are interrupting!" That did it. He hung his head, stuck out an angry lower lip, and scowled sideways at Earl. When Ma turned her attention to other things, Earl gave him a smug, defiant look.

"Straighten up and eat!" Harshness constricted Ma's thin face. Sitting opposite her husband, those blue hawk-like eyes were on all of them at the same time. Earl stiffened.

How's she do that? On his other side, three-year-old Ernie took a drink, hiccoughed, tensed, went beet red, gasped, and dropped the cup. Milk spilled down his shirt and splattered Earl's arm. The tin cup clattered across the floor. Struggling with food in his mouth, Ernie gagged, and grasped his brother's arm. Pleading, terror-filled eyes met Earl's; small nails dug in. Pa ran over, grabbed an arm, yanked Ernie from the bench, held him in front of himself, placed one big hand under the child's stomach, and thumped him on the back with the other. Food flew from Ernie's mouth and landed on the floor behind Earl. Ernie didn't cry, but he sure looked relieved. Pa set him on the bench beside Earl, then returned to his seat.

"Let it be a lesson, Son. Chew your food well, then swallow all of it before drinking. Shirley, get a mop. Edith, get

5

a rag. Alice, get him some water." Twelve-year-old Alice left the table, followed by fourteen-year-old Shirley, and Edith, thirteen. Earl glanced up and down the table. It was as if nothing had happened. All were eating, including Ma, whose expression hadn't changed. Ernie cleared his throat, then devoured everything on his plate. Food.... was important.

As the United States entered the Great Depression years, the Bensons got government commodities of flour, cheese, lard, powdered milk, powdered eggs, cornmeal, and sugar. Earl was glad they had chickens. He hated powdered eggs. Pa said it was a good thing they lived in America. Earl didn't understand what he meant, but it was fun to go downtown when there was a parade. Pa said it was the Fourth of July and that freedom was what they were celebrating, because Americans had worked hard, fought and, a great many died, to make it so.

The boys worked from the time they could walk, peddling newspapers in the snow, hauling them on a sled. One brother dragged the load along, while the others laid papers on porches. Often, they knocked, and hand delivered papers, which helped them keep the job for a long time. People on the route gave them hot cocoa, candy, or a treat when it was bitter cold.

"What a cute boy!" some said. Earl conceded that they could've been talking about Johnny or Ernie, too, maybe.

May 27, 1929, Helen Hazel, was born, making it more important for Mrs. Benson to keep things organized and clean.

"Had a bad dream. Don't feel good," said Earl one morn.

"You can't be sick! Get up and get busy with your chores, or I'll give you something to be sick about!" Hazel Benson kept after them. Money was important. Connecticut was a tobacco producer. Earl did what the boss called succoring, picking soiled or dried out bottom leaves off to make it grow better. Older boys harvested good leaves, a couple at a

6

time, starting at the bottom and moving higher as they became ready to pick.

Pa worked hard through the Great Depression, holding his position as a spinner at the mill, thankful his family had steady income. He didn't object to his wife pushing everyone to work hard, and realized how much better off his sons were compared to how things might've been had laws not changed. In the early 1800s, children as young as five worked long, hard hours in knitting mills in upper New York State. Yes, his sons had it easy. The Bensons were strong, stout, healthy and, for the most part, had minor bumps and scrapes.

Ma put poultices of tea leaves on infected cuts to draw out poison, and made poultices for colds and pneumonia. Earl's illnesses included mumps, measles, and chickenpox, but he almost died, December of 1929, at age seven, of double pneumonia. Seven-month-old Helen Hazel died of it on December 28th. Earl watched his mother's face harden and, within days after the tragic loss, it was as if baby Helen had never existed.

Accidents were another thing to struggle through. On a hot, sticky day in July, the boys begged to go swimming in Lake Guarda. Howard and Red promised to keep an eye on their younger brothers. It took a while, but Ma relented.

"Go..., but if you get in over your heads and drown, don't run to me for permission to go out there and do it again!"

At the lake, Howard, eleven, and Red, ten, good swimmers, headed for deep water, while the younger ones stayed near shore. The older boys treaded water and waggled fingers in the air.

"Hey, Earl!" said Red. "Look! We're touching bottom!"

"Yeah!" said Howard. "Ain't deep!" They turned their backs. Earl trusted them and, yearning to be on the raft anchored in deep water with the big kids, edged toward them.

They're touching, so it can't be deep. Wind stirred the water. In over his head, Earl panicked and fought to stay above choppy waves. Gagging, he cried out, gasped for air, reached for the surface, and sucked mouthfuls of water into his lungs.

"Howie! Red!" He screamed, as water filled his throat. Slipping below the surface, he clawed, fought, and sought for something, someone to grab on to. He surfaced several times, eyes wide, mind filled with terror, then sank into cool darkness.

Hands latched on..., hauled him upward....

"Fight..." Wrapped limply over slim shoulders, he was carried to shore. "Fight, boy!" She collapsed onto the sand, threw him over her lap, and pounded water from his lungs. "Breathe!" Everyone ran onto the beach.

"Somebody drowned!" Voices.... far away. Eyelids fluttered, then eyes opened wide. Earl coughed, spat water, shook, and fought for air. Brothers, everyone, gawked as he choked and gagged. Red-faced, he got a deep breath and started, of all things, bawling, which made him redder, but, then..., he saw his brother's faces. The crying ended because he remembered.... the Benson boys were tough.

Out of the stranger's lap, he gained footing, assured her he was fine, brushed sand off, and wiped annoying tears away. No thanks, nothing, he got away from there. By the time the brothers were home, he'd pulled himself together.

"Ain't letting Ma see me cry. No way!" No one told, knowing if they gave her the slightest clue something had gone awry, the trips to the lake would end.

Who was she? Earl never saw her again. What Howie had said was true. Angels looked after them. Earl decided there was a God in heaven, and an angel had been with him that day.

After the close call, Howard and Red made him learn to swim, and.... nearly drowned him in the process. He still swam much like a rock, but did make it all the way out to the raft.

Earl had many friends, the best being Donald Pelletier. If good times were to be had, Donnie was there. They climbed trees, a favorite pastime, in the yard and across the street in a deep wooded area. It was fun being high in the air. Earl loved to climb the tallest tree to the highest branch that would hold a boy his size, and see as far as he could see.

Ma hollered, "You fall out of there and break your legs, don't come running to me!"

The family had dogs, the current one a little bulldog. Earl watched, as Pa put Buster to sleep under one of Ma's washtubs.

Pa frowned as he said, "Earl, it's the only choice we have. Buster's old; he needs to be put down."

Buster was dead. Earl ran and climbed the tallest tree, all the way to the top, as tears filled his eyes.

"Oh, God..., I wish I was an eagle, so I could fly far away and never come back!" Where no one could see, he cried until it didn't hurt so bad. Not one to stay upset for long, he wiped his eyes, and sighed.

"Aw, Buster. I loved you so much!" Carrying sadness, grudges, or pouting wasn't in him. Smack in the middle of the family, it seemed he had to prove himself to older brothers and set a good example for the younger ones.

"I know you're in a better place, Buster," he whispered.

Soon, Johnny was walking around, down below, looking lost, as though he missed his best friend, too. Earl dropped leaves and twigs, grinning at their accuracy.

Johnny peered upward.

"I see you, Squirrely Early!" Moments later, they were off on another 'brothers are best buddies' adventure.

That night, Earl tossed and moaned, trapped in the horrible nightmare.

CHAPTER TWO

PREMONITION

Earl's mind screamed out, but the agonized pleas were not heard by the actual world.

"Let me outta here! No...! Help meee!" Fighting to escape the terror, he yelled, but his uncooperative mind captured the noise and buried it deep within itself. Fists clamped against sides, teeth clenched, fear shook him into consciousness. Sitting bolt upright, a gasp escaped into the dark, hot August night. Sweat and tears ran into and fell from wide-open blue eyes.

"No more," he whispered. Tensed fingers combed through scruffy, strawberry blonde hair recently shorn into a butch-cut, pulled down across freckled cheeks to a stubborn bottom lip, which curled downward under the pressure. Hands settled to blanket, fingers fidgeted with frayed edging. Always the same, the nightmare seemed real. In it was a small, dark room and they..., whoever they were..., would not let him out. Scaredy-cat? No. That much had been shown in eight years.

"I'm awake," he whispered. Wide eyes blinked, to be sure, and a couple of tears crept out. "It was the bad dream again." A stubby finger, poked into an eye, dislodged matter the sandman had left in the corner. The small bit was wiped onto the blanket. "I'm.... not.... afraid." Hands cupped wet cheeks and chin in calloused palms. Eyes stared into darkness.

"Benson boys are tough...." He peered at Howard's bed. Unable to see, knowing Howie was there, brought another tear.

"Why won't it go away? It's scary, and hurts, too, like

gettin' the wind knocked outta you. Gotta think of something else, so it won't come back. Bet Howie'd make it go away."

Howard, a no-nonsense type, could be counted on. He'd sat with Earl once before, long ago, when the dream had been new and terrifying. Earl rubbed his nose on the blanket.

"But what can Howie do about this? It's dark, and I might wake everyone up, trying to get over there." The idea of waking Howard passed almost as quick as it had come to mind. The thought of confinement in the small, dark room in the dream made him shudder.

"If God really loves me, why do I have to have this stupid dream? Am I.... that bad? Another tear fell. "It's always the same. Wish it would leave me alone! He peered upward.

"Please, God..., please..., make it go away!" He hadn't cried out, having learned long ago that it didn't help. No one had ever provided comfort, except Howard that one time. Fists clenched around the softness of the old blanket, then slammed down on top of sturdy legs.

"It's just a stupid, dumb dream! It's gone and can't hurt me anymore!" A shuddering yawn escaped from deep within. One last defiant tear trickled down, pausing a moment to dampen the depths of the dimple in his right cheek. It was wiped away, and then there were no more.

Crickets chirped out in the yard. Soothing comfort came from the sound of Howard's soft, even breathing. From the other side of Howard's bed came Red's snoring, interspersed with imperceptible mumblings, almost inaudible for once. Red could keep a deaf person awake when it came to sawing logs and talking out loud in the middle of the night, and there was hardly a night when he wasn't doing just that. A hard worker, not as dilligent as Howard, more follower than initiator, Red was an okay kind of brother Earl took lots of teasing from.

Ernest and John Henry, Jr. slept soundly next to Earl as a sliver of moonlight found its way into the dark room and sparkled faintly into half-closed eyes. Some night, not tonight, he'd understand the significance of the hellish vision. Quiet, caring not to awaken anyone, he lay down, snuggled into his pillow, tugged the blanket up to a determined chin, and filled his head with thoughts about going to the carnival.

"It'll be in Unionville soon. Sure hope Dad takes us." Memory counted nickels, dimes, and pennies saved, and hidden in a sock in a secret place. How would it be spent in that wonderland of rides and cotton candy? He yawned.

"Hope it's enough, 'cause I'm gonna have the best time I ever had in my whole life!"

Careful figuring and planning eased into dreaming a better dream, a child's dream, of a ferris wheel that went so high, so fast, it took his breath away, and left his stomach trying to catch up. Upon reaching its highest point, Earl reached for, and felt he might touch the stars twinkling in the late evening sky. It filled him with total satisfaction, complete happiness, and confident knowledge of belonging there.

Too soon, it ended, but, as he left the ride, music from a calliope's steam whistles beckoned. The sound, cheerful, pleasing, grew in prompting intensity as he made his way, darting through the milling crowd. Pace quickened, heart pounded, as he was drawn to the inspiring source.

There..., resplendent..., magnificent..., a magical carousel bedecked with multicolored steeds, whirling, prancing up and down under brilliantly lit canopy, galloping proudly to powerful strains from the most beautiful waltz melody he'd ever heard. Eyes glistening, heart racing, he chose a handsome, high-stepping stallion. Tongue-licked lips grinned, exposing not-too-perfect teeth, as he handed over his last ticket.

Carried into the warm night, Earl rode the carousel, imagining the steed, head held high, was real. Why, this trusty mount could take a person anywhere! Eyes squeezed shut, Earl wished, a daring, desperate wish.

He felt the magical transformation. Eyes flew open, the horse trembled, whinnied, and snorted. Points, sprouting from muscular withers, grew quickly, spreading upward and outward to become gossamer wings tinted with glittering rainbow hues.

The startling metamorphosis was almost complete. Empowered by desire, the Pegasus shook itself loose from the platform. Earl drew in a sharp breath as they flew into the night sky, higher than the heights the ferris wheel had gone to, soaring toward moon and stars, pure elation sweeping through mind and soul, entering through reins held tight in confident hands.

"No...!" he cried when, far below, music and carousel slowed, bringing the soaring duo gently to earth. The music ended. The carousel stopped. Letting go of the reins, Earl's arms wrapped about the charger's neck as it landed on the platform. Wings folded, then disappeared. Life left the great animal, and it was, once again..., a stone-cold wooden horse..., nothing more. Earl remained there for a few moments.

He slid off the now not so trusty mount, stepped from the platform, and shuffled away. Lights dimmed behind him. Shoulders slumped. Alone in the dark, quiet midway, he sighed, shoving hands deep into patched pockets.

"Shouldn't be anything...." Puzzlement crossed his face. One pocket, the right, was empty, but not the left. His hand closed around the discovery and pulled it out to reveal something strange and wonderful...., a hand full of coins, mostly silver quarters. Not one copper penny remained where there had been several before.

Softly, at first, then with increased intensity, lights and

music filled eyes and ears with luminosity and sound more stunning and much more colorful than before. Quickstep music came from a marching band whose members strutted by in shiny, black, high-topped boots and dazzling sequined magenta uniforms. Drums pounded; cymbals crashed. Trombones, cornets, flutes and fifes played brightly, filling him from head to toe with gleeful pleasure. Eyes wide with keen awareness, skin tingling with anticipation, he danced about as he realized he'd ride all of the rides as many times as his heart could desire. Best of all, he'd buy food! Hotdogs, candy apples, caramel corn, fresh hot roasted peanuts, and cotton candy!

Sensing the overwhelming aromas, tasting and savoring each delightful treat, he drifted farther into his dream.... with more than just a touch of a smile on his lips.

The next morning, after breakfast, Mrs. Benson dressed her boys in their best..., old, but clean. Most of their outfits weren't much to look at, but Earl was used to wearing hand-me-down knickers, bib-type overalls, and the way his mother tried to keep them spotless. The Bensons were proud of what they had. Although they bought clothing at the Salvation Army store, they were an average household, not well off, but not poor.

"Where we going?" asked Johnny as his bow tie was adjusted.

"Yeah," said Red, "it's not Sunday." Ma always made sure her children went to the Methodist church Sunday mornings.

"Hush now. Hurry up!" she said. "It's a surprise." They walked up Webster Street, then Plainville Avenue, crossed the tracks and the bridge. "There he is," she said. The boys jumped, trying to see what she saw, and spotted the horse.

"A Shetland Pony!" said Red. "Look! A man's taking

15

pictures!"

"Wow, Ma!" shouted Ernie. "Are we getting our pictures took?" He wiped his nose on the back of his hand, then whirled and skipped up the street.

"Not individual ones. He'll want a dollar to a dollar-and-a-half...." said Ma, but her boys were out of earshot.

The man, who traveled, town to town, with camera and brown and white pony, put two boys at at time on the horse. Earl and Ernie had their picture taken together.

Ernie and Earl Benson - About 1930

That night the boys told Pa about the surprise, and everyone laughed when he said, "That horse has had its picture taken so many times, with all the traveling they do. Can you imagine how many children have sat on his poor aching back? I'm surprised he didn't whinny and tell you to get off!"

Autumn and winter days were filled with all kinds of things for boys to do. Catch-a-fly-you're-up, kick the can, doc on the rock, ring-a-levio, hide-and-seek, and Fox and geese were favorites. Snow angels were everywhere. Snowball fights abounded, snow forts were constructed, and contests proved who could build the biggest, best snowman. Children on sleds and skates tore full speed down a slippery, hard-packed hillside on Gresch's farm and skittered across their solidly frozen pond. Barrel staves became skis with straps and thongs nailed on, and branches made great ski poles.

Having your own sled was a luxury not afforded. The children used their old toboggan a lot, as so many could pile on for a fun ride down a long slope. Fervent wishes for a sled for Christmas filled Earl's head. Even if it was for all of them, he'd consider himself lucky if it came. Christmas gifts wouldn't be much with nine, soon to be ten, children in the family.

December 17, 1930, Ma went to the hospital. Four days later she was home with a new brother for Earl and his siblings.

"His name's Robert, but you may call him Bobby." Earl stroked the downy top of little Bobby's head.

"Sure ain't much to look at with his red face scrunched up like that!" He went outside to do his own eight-year-old things.

Christmas morning, the five younger brothers got a Flexible Flyer, "From Santa, To the Benson Boys." A big gift, it was exciting to find under the tree. A nice present to share, clothing, socks, underwear, and a wonderful dinner at the solid oak dining table, made Christmas great.

Ma and Pa got a radio, their first. Despite hardships caused by the depression that gripped the nation, radio flourished and was a great way to relax and be entertained. Earl listened to 'Molly Goldberg' and shows the folks allowed. The Goldbergs, a Jewish family from New York, were hillarious. There was also 'Jimmy Durante,' 'The Amos and Andy Show,' and 'Buck Rogers.' Everyone listened at night, but the children couldn't listen in the day, as it took too much electricity. Pa came home, ate dinner, and listened to the news. Then, the family heard programs, like Earl's favorite, 'The Shadow.'

"Who knows what evil lurks in the hearts of men...? The Shadow knows!" was followed by sinister laughing, echoed by the boys, stiff fingers extended. They poked one another, put playful chokeholds around each others necks, and ended in a free-for-all, boys rolling on the floor admidst peals of laughter.

"Shush!" shouted Pa. Entertainment.... was important.

Earl saw movies at the town hall, Saturdays. Often, he waited outside with friend or brother. There were always a few around, pleading expressions, hopefully convincing and, often, after half a show was over, the attendant let a couple in free. Earl loved cartoons and saw the last half of many features.

Hunting.... was important, made money, and put food on the table. The brothers trapped small game, like silver, gray, and red fox, and shot squirrels. Earl became a good shot, though not supposed to fire the twenty-two, only the BB gun. Howard relented when Earl begged, and watched both Earl and Red like a hawk when they had the rifle. Muskrat trapping was a mainstay, furs sold to a furrier, with good skins fetching seventy-five cents each. Skunk skins paid less. Pelts with less white paid seventy- five cents or a dollar, but more white brought fifty cents, or a quarter. Earl helped with skinning. Howard made wedge-type boards, pointed in front. Hides were slid on, inside-out, with the back ends tacked taut to stretch them. Insides were scraped, then the hides dried.

Neighbors.... were important. An old farmer, Mister Moses, lived nearby, and had a sawmill, farm, and land with brooks running through it. Battles were ongoing, as boys trespassed and gave him a hard time.

One morning, after a rainy night, they raided his melon patch. The field was soggy, but the boys marched in, searching for ripe watermelons. Determined to outdo everyone, Earl found the biggest one, in the middle of the field, perfect, begging to be taken. Donnie hooted and whistled.

"Can't run fast or get through the fence quick if you take that one, and what if Old Man Moses sees us?" Earl tried not to think about that as he stumbled along, fumbling with the huge melon. Mud sucked at his shoes, trying to pull them from his feet. Donnie giggled as he held his melon at the edge of the field. The others, with their's, were beyond the fence, headed for the woods.

"Drop them damn melons!" Mister Moses, moving fast, yelled, and shook a fist at them. Seeing the double-barreled shotgun, Earl slid..., and fell flat on his face. Melon flew from slick hands, rolled through the muck, and stopped. Mud-covered, head to toe, he jumped up, threw himself onto the elusive fruit, scooped it up, tried to stand, slipped, fell flat on his face, got his feet under him, found solid ground, and bolted for the fence. Donnie was suffering a fit of hysterical laughing on the other side, as he nearly lost it again.

The laughter stopped.... Donnie's expression changed.

"Holy macaroni! Run, Earl! He's coming!" Donnie sprinted for the woods.

Earl rolled the melon under the barbed wire, stepped between two stands, snagged his shirt on the sharp barbs, yelled, "Owhh, jeepers!" tore loose, scrambled away, scooped up the melon, and was running..., but so was Mister Moses!

"No!" shouted Donnie from behind a tree. "Don't shoot! Whoa, don't drop it!" Earl ran like never before. Moses hollered, then fired off a shot.

"Thievin' bastards!" The blast pushed Earl into full motion. Melon tight to chest, he put as much distance between the fence and himself as possible, but...,

"Ka-blamm!" The other barrel fired. Earl yelped and

limp-dashed into the woods. Mister Moses reached the fence, shook his fist, swore, and..., gave up the pursuit.

Deep in the woods, the boys broke out a couple of pocket knives. Earl savored the moment, enjoying the sweetest melon ever grown. Feeling his backside, he winced.

"Dang! And I'll probably catch it at home, worse than I caught it from Moses!"

He tried sneaking into the house, but Ma was all over his case upon seeing the torn shirt, muddy clothes, and shoes.

"And just where have you been?" Earl looked boldly from under mud-caked eyebrows.

"Fell down.... alongside the creek."

"Oh...?" She spun him around, noting the holes. More than once, she'd picked rock salt from backsides and, about that time, she spotted Red sneaking Johnny and Ernie through the back door. That did it. Hazel decided her boys needed extra jobs to keep them busy and out of mischief.

CHAPTER THREE

EGGSHELLS

Ma knitted and crocheted, for family, and to sell. Doilies, potholders, dishclothes, booties, bonnets, for her boys to take door-to-door. She rigged a tray, supported by a neck strap, carried in front of the wearer, then loaded it. The boys had to talk to people because if they didn't sell most of the wares..., Ma talked to them when they got home. Earl learned the business and could count change at an early age.

There was still time for fun and, yes..., fun was important. During his ninth winter, Earl had a significant fender bender, sledding down Greschs' hill on his stomach with Ernie clinging to his back. Unable to steer, he was headed for a huge oak.

"Get off Ernie!" Ernie rolled clear. Earl hit the tree.... so hard his ears rang like bells in a church tower. He came away with a two inch gash in his scalp. Ernie trotted over.

"Hey, Earl! You're bleeding all over your coat!" Someday he'd inherit it, and blood would ruin it. He wiped his nose on a snow-covered sleeve, and stared at his older brother.

"How come you didn't get off?"

Earl gave him his best dirty look then sent him to get Red and Howard, who loaded him onto the sled, then took turns pulling, with Johnny and Ernie close behind. Earl groaned.

"Man..., it hurts so bad!"

"Is Earl gonna die, Howie?" asked Ernie. Johnny punched Ernie's arm.

"Don't say that! Earl ain't dying, dummy!" Ernie hit

back.

"Don't call me a dummy, Johnny!"

"Well, then, don't be acting like a dummy, dopey!" Johnny jabbed Ernie harder. Grabbing the arm, Ernie collapsed onto both knees, lower lip out, tears filling his eyes.

"Howie...!" he bellowed. Johnny's hitting me and calling me dopey!" Howard handed the tow rope to Red, stepped back and, without a word, swatted both boys upside their heads. That got them both going. Howard took the tow rope from Red.

Ernie gave Johnny a smug, defiant look.

At the house, Howard reported the accident.

Ma ran out, took a look, said, "Oh, my God! Now what've you done?" ran inside, came out with coat, purse, and rag, slapped the rag onto Earl's bloody head, then, talking to herself, hands waving about, directed the procession to the doctor's office where he put his patient back together with staple-like clamps.

Head throbbing, Earl rode home on the sled, then sat on the back steps as Howard and Red worked on the sled's steering.

"There, brother!" said Howard. "Problem's gone. Take 'er down any hill, slicker than snot on a doorknob, and she won't get away from you again. I promise." Earl winced.

"Thanks, but..., I wish you could fix my head so it'd stop hurting." Howard clapped a hand onto Earl's shoulder.

"Don't worry, brother! It'll stop aching pretty soon." Earl noticed that he did not say, "I promise," this time. Red whistled sharp, high to low, hand making a low dive from overhead.

He grinned, then said, "I heard the tree you hit.... fell over after we left! Earl the pearl, you have the hardest head in Unionville!" Times like this made Earl realize.... even Red cared. He winced and grinned at his older siblings. They were good brothers, feared little, and were considered by reputation to be some of the toughest boys around.

There was one problem in town, though, everyone knew about. Robinson. Rotten Robbie, town drunk, six feet tall, like an Amazon giant to Earl, cleared his throat constantly, hawking, spitting, and making enough noise so people heard him all over the place if anywhere within earshot.

Going to town, Earl rode the old bicycle the boys shared across the only bridge. The span was huge, with sidewalks on both sides for pedestrians, forty feet above the rushing water of the Farmington River. Riding on the sidewalk, off the busy street, Earl saw Robinson coming, and realized the man was drunk. Keeping it steady, Earl steered aside to get by but, suddenly, the drunk's huge hands were on the bike. With an astounded Earl aboard, Robinson held it chest high.

Foul, inebriated fumes encompassed Earl's face, as the old sot said, "Now I've got you, ya little crapper!"

"What're you doing? Put me down," screamed Earl. Robinson's sneer was wicked.

"What am I doing? Hah! I'm throwing you and your ugly bike in the river. I'm drowning your miserable butt! That's what I'm doing!" His red face scrunched into a horrible, glaring mass of wrinkles and scars as he raised the bicycle higher.

"No! Put me down! I ain't never done nothing to you! Why're you doing this? Put me dow...owwn!" he screamed as Robinson shook the bicycle, then lifted it higher.

"Hey..., asshole!" Earl heard the shout. Robinson lowered the bike, and stared up the street. Brows knotted, piglike eyes stared at Earl, then up the street again as Howard ran all-out, toward them. Howard's voice, changing with becoming a teenager, jumped back and forth and up and down as he yelled.

"Put him down! Idiot! Put my brother down!" Howard was older, almost shorter than Earl, but much tougher.

Robinson, Earl in one gigantic hand, grabbed the front of Howard's shirt with the other. Howard hauled off and kicked him in the shins.

"Let him go, you old buzzard!" Well-aimed blows made the giant release his grip.

"Owww... dang!" cried Earl, landing in a crumpled heap atop the bicycle, which had fallen into the street. A big truck came at him. Untangling himself, he jumped out of the way, then lifted the bike onto the sidewalk. The intoxicated Amazon turned and grabbed for him.

Howard, in that God-awful, shrill-high to pounding-low voice, screamed, "Run, Earl! Pete's sake! Run!" Earl scrambled onto the bicycle, peddled for all his heart and soul were worth, and stopped after reaching the end of the bridge. Straddling the bike, he realized he was shaking like a leaf.

"Oh, God," he gasped, trying to catch his breath, "please don't let Howie get hurt!" Slamming a hard fist into the palm of his other hand, he yelled, "Get him, Howie! Hit him! Knock him on his butt!" Robinson stumbled about, holding onto Howard's shirt. So thin, Howard twisted about, then downward with a quick jerk, and slipped right out of it.

Quicker than a sneeze, he grabbed the shirt, yanked it from Robinson's grasp, and yelled, "Dumb son-of-a-bitch! You got me mad now!" Robinson had brought a hornets' nest down around his ears. The barrage of pounding fists dealt him made Earl see what resembled a giant zombie being attacked by a pygmy. In a lightning-fast move, Howard jumped up, smashed a right hook into the drunk's nose, then ducked and delivered a fearsome left, catching the ogre below the belt. Earl watched, open-mouthed, as Howard slammed home a few more licks, grabbed his shirt, covered with tire tracks and badly torn from where it had fallen onto the pavement, and ran. Howard slowed, then trotted over to his brother.

Drenched in sweat, breath coming in deep, shuddering gasps, he said, "What're you still doing here? Let's go!" Earl grinned at his brother.

"Man, Howie, you're a true champion, a genuine hero, just like Buck Rogers!" He pushed the bicycle as they walked up Webster Street. "Yup, How..., you got guts, and I'm glad you're my brother." He stopped and pulled on Howard's arm forcing him to look at him.

"Howie..., why'd Robinson grab me? He was gonna kill me, I know he was, and I ain't never done nothing to him." Howard didn't answer, but Earl caught him grinning like a sly fox as they started walking again.

"Earl, this wouldn't have happened if you didn't look so darn much like your older brothers." No matter how many times asked, Howard nor Red ever told Earl what they had done to Robinson to make him go after their younger brother like that. Howard had saved the day, that's what mattered, and Earl knew he would always be able to look up to him if things got rough.

Things got rough. On a warm spring day in 1932, Earl's world turned upside down. His parents had been fighting for quite some time and his nightmare was back. He walked home from school that awful day.

"Maybe if I was a better kid, they wouldn't fight and the dream would go away." Nearing the house, he spotted Ma with a strange man in the front yard. Unseen, Earl approached, innocent, unaware, looked at them, through them, and..., it didn't register. Then, eyes widened in disbelief, he looked again and stumbled.

"They're.... kissing...." Quickly, quietly, he backed up, turned, and walked away. Filled with sadness and shame for her and the whole family, he hung his head.

"Why's she doing this?" Eyes squeezed back a flood of tears that tried to fill them. "How can she do this!" Worn shoes stomped and kicked against the sidewalk, then at clumps of dirt and stones, as he stormed into the woods.

"God! I wish she hadn'ta done that! Dang it! Whole mess is her fault. She's my mother, I'm 'sposed to love her, but I hate her! Even if Dad still cares, nothing'll ever be the same."

Love was hard enough to come by, as it was, in the Benson home. Earl couldn't remember his folks expressing it to one another, nor to their children. He was unaware of being hugged or comforted when hurt or when the bad dream scared him. Somehow, love had become an assumption for the whole family.

"You don't have to say it, so maybe it's still there, somewhere." He paused, and peered up at a slim shaft of light that shone down through the tree tops.

"God..., if that's not You up there..., I hope it's my angel. You see what's happening down here..., don't You...? Please...," he begged, choking back a sob, "please..., don't let bad things happen. It hurts...." Hot tears cascaded down his cheeks. "It.... just hurts too much...! You just gotta love us and make things right!" Eyes squeezed shut, then opened. The light shimmered bright, then dimmed.

"You.... You really can hear me...." Earl lowered his head, brushed away the tears, then walked on.

Deep in the woods, he voiced his frustration.

"Fighting's worse..., arguments happen at night after we're in bed. Dad accuses Ma of running around. Ma screams, calls him names I never heard of, and she usually has the last word..., then..., the next day..., nobody says nothin' to no one about it. That bastard had no right kissing her! I love Dad..., should've gone and told him about the filthy creep!"

Remembering his parent's last confrontation, he realized his father knew what was going on, but that relieved only a small portion of the heavy burden.

"We walk around her house like we're on eggshells. Don't gotta be told to get out and do chores, either, 'cause everyone wants to be as far away from her as possible. Ain't fair, how she treats us, and look at her! Closet full of store-bought dresses and stuff.... With the money she gets from Dad and us kids, she's living way better than the rest of us."

Hands shoved deep into pockets, Earl wandered through the woods, thoughts pressing forward to cross his lips.

"We wear patches on patches, on hand-me-downs. Dad's got nothing nice to wear, except his suit for church and funerals. I know we have a big family, lots of people do, so why's Ma so selfish? 'Cause she only cares about herself..., that's why!" He sat on a stump, feet not quite touching the ground, leaning forward, rough elbows atop knees, wet chin cupped in hands.

"Fights started about the time Bobby was born, when I was eight. Maybe that's it. She's tired of having so many kids." He sighed. "Sometimes..., I wish we all belonged to someone else." Another thought shoved its way across his lips.

"Wonder if she even cares anymore?"

Nights later, he climbed into bed, and faced the wall.

"Does she know I saw her kiss him?" His mother had become a strange, greedy, vicious woman, in his eyes and heart. He didn't know her anymore and wondered if somehow she felt his changed attitude. He folded the pillow about his ears.

"Has she been meaner just to me?" He shut his eyes.

"No..., she's been harder on the rest of the family, too."

Things did not improve. His parents split up and Pa moved out. No surprise, but Earl did not expect what happened next. Bounding into the house one day, he stopped short. Suitcases sat by the front door. In the kitchen, Ma talked in hushed tones to Edith, Shirley and Alice. When he entered, they clammed up. Ma faced him, and touched a hand to her freshly shortened curls.

"Go round your brothers up. Tell them to get in here and wash up." Earl studied his sisters' faces.

Something's wrong.... The girls shuffled about, no one doing anything in particular, just going though lots of meaningless motions. Tears glistened in Alice's eyes.

"What's going on?" He stared out at the luggage, then turned to see his mother glaring at him.

"Just do what I told you.... Now!" Earl looked beyond her and saw eighteen-year-old Kenneth headed up the basement steps, old suitcases clasped in each hand. Kenneth spotted Earl, and gave him a look that sent cold shivers racing along his spine. Beads of sweat ran down the sides of Earl's face.

Something's happening.... Kenny's look says so.... it's happening right now..., and it's happening to me! Mouth open, mind racing, heart tumbling down a sheer cliff wall, he froze. His mother stepped toward him.

"God's sake, boy! Do as you're told! Move!" Her open hand struck the side of his face.

"Owww! I'm going!" Earl fled out the back door and, blinded by tears, stumbled down the steps.

Later, faces scrubbed, Howard, Red, Johnny, Ernie, and Earl sat in the front room, waiting for God in heaven knew what. Pa's car pulled up. He got out, but didn't approach the house.

"C'mon guys!" Kenneth said, too cheerfully. Grabbing suitcases, he started out the door. "Let's get these bags out to the car." Earl and Red looked at Howard. Johnny and Ernie stayed put on the couch. Howard nodded.

Struggling with suitcases, they made their ways down the steps and over to the back of the car. Ernie ran to Pa.

"I know! We're going on a trip! A big one! Are we going to New York State to see Aunt Min? Aunt Min's your sister, huh, Pa? Are we going there to live with you?" John Henry looked up at his wife, who stood on the porch holding baby Robert. He gave her a thoroughly disgusted look.

"You haven't even bothered to tell them..., have you?" Hazel shifted her child from one hip to the other and glared.

"They.... are your sons," she said in a strange voice. "You tell them." Earl's eyes widened. He looked from one to the other. Pa's voice was quiet, concerned.

"No, Ernie.... Come on, boys. Let's go." Howard and Red followed Johnny and a wide-eyed Ernie into the back of the car. Earl stood on the sidewalk, back to them, eyes brimming.

He looked up into his father's sad, much older face and, just loud enough for only him to hear, whispered, "I love you, Dad..., can't we all just stay here?" John Henry raised agonized eyes toward heaven, then gazed down at his son. For a long moment he looked as if the weight of the whole world sat on his shoulders. He sucked in a deep breath.

"Earl, this is the only choice we've been given, so we have to make the best of it. You'll only be gone a little while, then I'll get you back..., I promise.... You know I keep my word, Son."

Earl couldn't feel anything for a second, then..., he felt his soul being swept away by a raging river, the horrible, rushing sound of it filling his head.

"G..Gone...? Where...? You..., you can't be saying this...! Dad..., no! I don't want to go! Please...!" he said, choking in an effort not to cry or raise his voice above a desperate whisper. "I'll do all of the work around here..., and I'll be good..., I will...! I promise!" John Henry gripped Earl's shoulder for a moment. He looked deep into blue eyes, then ran his trembling hand over his son's strawberry blonde hair. His voice caught.

"You need to be strong now, for Johnny and Ernie. I... Uh, get into the car now."

"Please, Dad.., just give me a chance to keep my promise!" Breath sobbed in Earl's lungs for three deep, agonized gasps. Lower lip trembling, his voice cracked as he said, "Oh, God, Dad, please don't make us go...., please...." Pa's firm look silenced him. John Henry entered the car and stared straight ahead. Earl glared at his mother, then screamed.

"It's not his fault. It's yours!" She returned a brief, icy countenance, then turned and clicked into the house. The screen door slammed. Earl's worn shoes scuffed against the sidewalk.

"How can she do this?" He got in only after he'd wiped the tears from his eyes, and forced calmness upon his face. It was quiet. Too quiet. Pa started the car. It left the curb. Earl eyed his brothers' faces. Fighting to be brave, they couldn't look at him or one another as Pa drove down Webster Street.

Earl stared out the back window at the house he'd grown up in. Kenneth and his sisters stood on the porch, waving, faces grim. At the bottom of the hill, Pa turned left on to Plainville Avenue. Earl turned and sat forward on the edge of the seat.

Where we going? He studied Pa's face as they crossed the tracks, then the bridge, and passed through Unionville. He knew it was tearing his father apart to have to do this, though what this was.... he didn't know.

Soon the car pulled into a long drive, lined gracefully with trees along each side. Long branches, wrapped in green foliage, formed a beautiful canopied archway above. The car stopped in front of wrought iron gates through which Earl saw red brick buildings in the distance that reminded him of a picture he'd seen at school of a college campus. He watched as a thin, old gentleman opened the gates. The man wore a black watchcap and gloves even though it wasn't cold.

"Hello there, young fella!" said Mister Benson. He always said that to old people, but had told his boys they couldn't unless they were at least somewhere near the person's age because it would be disrespectful. He asked questions Earl could not quite hear. The man pointed at a building, waved them through, smiling, as if he knew them.

"I've heard of this place," Howard whispered. "It's an orphanage and home for destitute kids." Red nudged Howard as their father parked in front of a vine-covered structure.

"We can still make a run for it, right?" He looked hard at Howard, as did Earl, Johnny and Ernie. Howard frowned.

"If we run, they'll just catch us and haul our butts right back here." He opened the car door, held it for them, and said, "Sit tight, guys. I've heard this isn't a bad place, so let's make the best of it and, remember..., us Benson boys are tough!"

FOUR

GOD DOESN'T TALK TO PEOPLE

And they were tough, except Ernie. Clinging to Pa's leg, he pitched one hell of a fit. It was all Earl could do to be strong like he knew he had to be, when his own lip was trembling.

"Ernie, you've never cried like this." Pa peeled Ernie off, and handed him to Howard who held on tight and tried to soothe his brother as he kicked and screamed. Their father entered the building, then returned with a middle-aged man who introduced himself while Ernie sobbed against Howard's shoulder.

John Henry left his sons at the orphanage..., promised he would visit..., then simply drove away.

Earl muddled through the home's routine for the next few weeks in a daze. Guilt and shame from being in a strange place with a bunch of kids nobody wanted was difficult to handle.

"I don't belong here. I want to go home!"

The orphanage was regimented in its daily schedule; the boys did as they were told and were expected to care for themselves. They were fed, provided with clean clothing, schooled, and controlled, all within the confines of the establishment. There were no chores, and they were kept busy with soccer and games. Earl liked baseball. The Benson boys loved sports, played well, and were usually picked first when teams were formed.

July 27, 1932 was Earl's tenth birthday, months since the five brothers had arrived at the orphanage. He'd adjusted, was laughing and smiling like he used to before being brought here, but things were still rough at times.

A stressful day left him tired and homesick. Pressure built until that night, he prayed so hard his head, and his heart, ached. He wept, broken-hearted, muffling shuddering sobs into his pillow. Exhaustion brought uneasy sleep wrought with tossing and moaning. In the middle of the night, the nightmare returned, worse than it had ever been.

"No...!" He fought to break through darkness.

"Let me outta here!" Unable to breathe, he struggled to catch his breath. When he did, he screamed again.

"Let me out! Let me outta here!"

Desperate pleas were heard. Howard stroked Earl's hair and whispered, but Earl flailed arms and legs, trying to beat through the walls and door of a tiny, cold, pitch-black room.

"Earl!" Howard's voice broke through, and Earl felt strong arms about him. He was hugged tight to his brother's chest, and rocked back and forth.

"Shush...! Hush...! It's okay...! Hey, you..., wake up, brother! It's all right, Earl..., I'm here.... You're okay!" Eyes opened and blinked a couple of times. Hot tears splashed down onto freckled cheeks. Earl looked miserably up at Howard.

"Oh, How-Howie! I... wanna go ho...home!" Howard squeezed him tighter.

"I know, brother..., I know...." Howard pressed his cheek against the top of Earl's head. From the depths of his soul, he sighed, then whispered, "We have to pray it will happen soon."

"I'm not prayin' anymore, Howie! God doesn't answer me. I can't be strong for Johnny and Ernie, either. If God loved us..., He wouldn't let bad things happen!" Howard took him by the shoulders and shook him hard.

"No, Earl! Listen to me! What's to be will be. You take things in stride, one thing at a time..., one day at a time. God's got reasons for everything that happens. When things are bad, you do your best to make them better..., and you never stop praying!" He gave Earl a gentle shake.

"Remember, I told you before, even the angels are busy, so you've got to learn patience. God doesn't talk to most people. Things just happen and sometimes they take time. We're in His hands..., and we just have to trust Him. He has lots of us to look after, and that's why He made guardian angels. Then..., even they're overloaded at times, so.... you have to learn patience, brother...! Think of good things every night before you go to bed, and I promise..., things will get better."

A few nights later, Earl folded his hands. "God..., when are we going be a family again? Why are You doing this? Do we have to stay here forever? When do we get to go home? Do You.... do You even listen to anything a dumb kid like me has to say...?" Answers didn't come, much as he wanted them to. He never let anyone see or hear him pray. He knew he must be strong and set a good example for Johnny and Ernie who slept on cots not far from his own.

Earl watched his younger brothers..., listened for their sadness. Neither had slept alone before. They'd barely managed the sudden change in their lives. At first, Howard had spent a few nights sitting in the dark with them clinging and crying while he tried to soothe away broken, homesick hearts. Torn between his need to be tough or comforted, it was nearly impossible for Earl to stay in bed. But even now, as it had been then, he toughed it out, remained abed, and got over it. He didn't cry easily after that, and knew not to get hopes up, only to have them dashed. Pondering Howard's advice, he came to a conclusion.

35

"My guardian angel is a beautiful, nice lady, everything Ma's not." He began praying each night.

His mother's visits were rare. Pa came often, but wasn't permitted to take his sons for rides or to a carnival. Earl held tight to his good dream, hoping someday it would come true. At night, fearing the nightmare might return, he clutched the reins of the strong Pegasus and escaped into the star-filled, sweet dream sky and, soon..., forgot the bad dream.

The boys took their own baths, then dressed in provided outfits. Dressers by their beds held clothing and essentials. Howard and Red had deodorant powder in their's.

"How come you guys get powder, and we don't?' asked Earl. He'd noticed that Howard, careful about appearance, used powder sparingly, but sufficiently. Earl pulled on his socks.

"Red's not like Howie. He dumps powder all over and doesn't give a hoot about how he looks."

Red swung about, and grabbed a shirt from his drawer.

"Half-pints don't get powder!" He buttoned his shirt. It hung lopsided, so he rebuttoned it. Johnny fell onto Red's bed.

"You can't even button your shirt right, so how come you get powder and we don't?" Red pounced on Johnny, who squealed as his brother tickled him. Earl jumped into it.

"We don't get deodorant powder, 'cause we smell so good, and Howie and Red smell soooo bad!"

Suddenly, Ernie shrieked, "I want some duhodorunt powder, too!" He giggled, and piled headlong into his brothers. It was the first time he'd laughed since coming here.

Pounding on Red, he shouted, "Give me some powder, you big smelly bully! I want some right now!" Howard pulled them all apart and got them settled down.

"Knock it off," he said, trying to keep a straight face, "or we'll all be in trouble with a great big capital T!"

36

Mouth open, Earl stared at the doorway...,

"Dad...."

John Henry gazed at his sons. They had been away from home nearly a year. He trembled. Eyes glistened.

"Well..., somehow I just knew when I got up this morning that our guardian angels were all on duty. Now don't just stand there with your bare faces hanging out. Let's go home!" Gleeful sons smothered him with a giant hug, and their father finally whispered what Earl had waited a lifetime to hear.

"God...! I love you all..., so much!" Earl felt tears on his cheek, and grinned, unsure if they were his own or Pa's.

Or..., maybe, my guardian angel's crying because she's happy Pa kept his promise. Earl touched the wet spot.

Thanks, God. I'll never stop praying..., not ever again!

Smile bright, he joined his brothers as they hugged their father tighter, and chorused, "We love you, too, Pa!"

They piled into Pa's Overland, a bench seat convertible sedan that sat high in the air, had two long seats, front and rear, fold-down seats on each side for extra passengers, big wheels with wooden spokes. Headed for home, Earl was singing.

"This is the best ride I've taken in my whole life!"

Ma and Pa were back together and, somehow, things returned to the way they were before the trouble had started. Earl wasn't paying attention to what went on at home, anyway. He was too busy being a kid, happy to be home. With all he was doing, there wasn't time to think about serious matters. He had things to do and places to go. The boys rode happily with their father out into the countryside, sometimes to Collinsville or Winstead and, one day, a carnival. John Henry couldn't afford much, but somehow had enough spare change stashed for his boys to spend on a ride or two.

Earl ran full speed everywhere, and sometimes rode one

of their old bicycles around town. There weren't enough hours in the day to fullfill his need for freedom.... freedom to be with friends, go where he wanted, almost anytime he wanted....

Hazel Benson put her boys to work and kept their time occupied. In school, everyone in band class had to have an instrument. Members of the family who showed interest usually had one. Ma made payments of a dollar per week on a clarinet for Earl when he was in fifth grade. He enjoyed playing, was enthusiastic about the progress he'd made with the band, but times got rough again, it couldn't be afforded, and he lost it. It wasn't fair, but things did get better after awhile.

Hazel Benson loved music, played piano well, and tap danced. Shirley, nineteen, was a terrific singer with a voice that sent shivers dancing along Earl's spine.

"Shirley Girl," he said, "you're good enough to sing on the radio!" At times, she sounded so sad it tugged on his heart. Other times, her singing was strong and happy. Edith had turned eighteen and enjoyed piano as much as her mother did.

Of Red's wailing away on the harmonica, Earl said, "Sometimes you sound like an old hound dog who's chased a poor, old cat up a tree."

"And you sound like the poor old cat!" said Red. Fourteen, he was good about not taking anything too seriously.

Almost twelve..., almost was important..., Earl played saxophone, and did his best to keep this instrument, no matter what. He studied hard and played well when it came down to it.

Then there was Johnny, who, at the age of ten, was the good-looking one in the family..., well liked by girls.

"Later on," Ma said, "he's going to be a lady's man." Johnny took a liking to the drums..., and was good at that, too.

When Kenneth, twenty-one, was around he played fiddle, mostly country and western cowboy tunes, but almost any kind of serious music, too. Oh, how he played! Laying that fiddle over his back, on top of his head or between those lanky legs, he played like a fool. It was something to hear!

Three-year-old Bobby was too young to put two-cents worth into the musical pot, not that he didn't try, for those with no instruments were given pot lids to bang on with metal and wooden spoons. Earl considered him a mama's boy, and wasn't around him much, with the age spread. Ernie, like Red, had always been kind of laid back, and not too matter-of-fact. He took lots of ribbing from Earl, as did Johnny, but, home from the orphanage, Ernie was different. He fussed and whined when brothers teased and, now, he didn't want to bang on a stupid pot lid. Earl sighed.

When's he gonna toughen up?

The Bensons owned a rooster, and chickens, which might have been enough to keep any rooster contented and busy, but not this one. Roo, a white leghorn, chased everybody, and his favorite target was Ma. He chased the woman back and forth between the outhouse and the back door, never missing a beat, and the boys tormented him without mercy, so he was twice as mean and feisty. Roo had an uncanny knack for spotting Ma just when she'd gotten midway between the house and the outhouse and, sometimes..., she didn't make it out of the toilet.

One day, Earl and Red heard her out back, shrieking, "Hey in there! Fer cripes sake, get out here and chase this damn, stupid rooster away!" Earl winced.

"Her again.... always yelling for someone to come and rescue her." He sighed. Earl and Red were doing homework at the kitchen table. Red glanced dolefully across the table at Earl.

"Yup..., Roo's got Ma pinned in the toilet again." Earl jumped up, then stared out the window at the outhouse. Red followed. Sure enough, Roo had Ma cornered and was strutting around and around the old outhouse..., which reminded Earl of a movie he'd seen where Indians had surrounded the pioneers' wagons. Fingers stiff, he patted his lips, then poked Red in the ribs. A silent war dance began around the table.

Earl couldn't count the times Roo had surprised people. They'd turn and..., there he was, beating wings, and spurring.

Red and Earl continued the almost quiet dance. Things were not quiet out back. Roo strutted his stuff, circling, waiting for the door to open while Ma yelled obscenities from within. Red returned to the window, rested elbows on the sill, and studied the outhouse. Earl hopped around the table. Ma started with the intolerable screaming. Red looked at Earl.

"Huh...! Looks like she's real scared this time. Reckon we ought to get on out there, brother?" Earl stopped hopping, joined his brother, and sighed as he leaned on the window ledge.

"Yeah..., I s'pose so." Red handed him a mop from the corner, then took a broom for himself and started for the door. Earl grinned and jabbed Red's backside.

Red turned, faced his assailant, said, "En garde!" and they jousted for a few moments, shoving each other back and forth across the polished wood floor.

At Red's command, they stood at attention, saluting each other, until he said, "Ready..., set..., go!"

Barreling out the back door, they jumped from the porch, skipped the steps, and landed in the driveway. Red kept his footing, but Earl rolled once, then stood wildly waving the mop.

"Roo, get outta here!" yelled Red. "Leave Ma alone! Stupid rooster!" Clouds of dirt, dust, and feathers filled the air, as he swept after the old cock.

Earl took after Roo with the mop, hollering, "Scram outta here! Git going, ya dumb old bird!" He laughed. "Oh yeah, real dumb. This bird's dumb like a fox! Move it Roo! Go on, you crazy old ball of feathers!"

Johnny and Ernie heard the commotion and now were on the back porch, sides held, doubled over, laughing themselves silly. Between their hoots, Earl and Red's yelling, Ma's shrieks, hens squawking, dog barking, and feathers, dust and dirt flying all over the place..., Earl's grin was ear to ear.

"Good ole Roo.... This is so much fun!"

CHAPTER FIVE

DO AS I SAY, NOT AS I DO

At some point, Earl realized... having older brothers around to keep you out of trouble might be a good thing. The boys were continually learning what to do and, most definitely, what not to.

One bright afternoon, he stood behind the garage smoking a cigarette. He inhaled.

Folks are gone..., don't see anyone around. He exhaled. Nobody can see me here.

Nobody could see him, but Kenneth smelled the smoke. He crept up from behind and grabbed Earl by the neck.

"What in God's name do you think you're doing?" This caused Earl to jump straight into the air and nearly have a heart attack. Kenneth grabbed an ear, and hauled him into the house.

"I can't believe you're smoking, especially after the last time!" He pushed Earl down onto a stool. "Doggone it, Earl! You sure are persistant." He thought a moment. "You really want to smoke, brother?" Earl shrugged. Kenneth reached into a pocket, and withdrew a cigar.

"Smoke this. Soon's you're finished, we'll see how bad you wanna smoke." Earl stared at him.

"Hold on, Kenny...! I was just trying to see what it's like!" He grimaced. Dumb! He knows you've smoked before.

"And liars go straight to hell, too, brother...," Kenneth moved to put the cigar between pursed lips. "so don't even begin to try your lame stories on me." He struck a kitchen match along the edge of the table. The match flared bright, then burned steadily as he puffed until he got the end of the cigar to burn in a tight, hot red coil. He held it in front of himself and blew out the match, filling the air with mixed odors of burned sulfer and tobacco. Handing it over, he grinned.

"Here you go, hotshot." Earl glared into his brother's eyes as he took the cigar.

"Think ya gotta teach me a lesson, Kenny? Well, go ahead and try!" A drag on the stogie closed his windpipe. In a fit of furious coughing, he fought to keep his insides from abandoning him. The top of his head was coming off..., he was sure of it, but he caught his breath and rasped, "Great cigar, brother! Thanks!" He inhaled again, but not deeply.

Ain't breaking me. Not today. Not ever. Who's he think he is, anyway? President Roosevelt? Earl grinned up at his brother. Kenneth laughed.

"Hardheaded little turd, ain'tcha? Must run in the family, huh?" His face hardened as he continued, "Well..., that's okay. I've been up this road with Howard, and back down it again with Red." Kenneth sat on a stool, and faced him with a look that made Earl realize just how determined his oldest brother was.... Yup..., there was a goose cooking somewhere..., but..., Earl smiled and made a promise to himself.

I'll smoke again..., just.... well..., maybe not today. Kenneth made him smoke the cigar, and Earl was a bit green by the time it was down to his brother's satisfaction. Kenneth was oldest, and had to set the younger brothers straight, even if he didn't set good examples himself. The rule was do as I say, not as I do. Fact was, Kenneth was a real corker at times.

One time in particular, he was in the basement with his brothers and a couple of neighborhood boys, when he decided to teach them about electricity. He took one of Pa's steel fishing rods over to the ceiling light fixture, unscrewed the bulb, played hot potato for a moment, then looked around at the boys.

"Now, listen children, and you shall hear..., the shocking story of Paul Revere."

"Paul Revere?" they chorused. He had their attention.

"Here we go!" said Kenneth. He stepped under the socket, pretended to jam the steel tip of the rod into it, jumped up and down, did a shaking jig, and let out a yell.

"Oh! It's got me! I'm being eeelectrocutionated!" He stood still, rolled and crossed his eyes, then said, "Just kidding.... See...? I can't get shocked. Here, I'll prove it. C'mere, Earl, grab my hand." Earl frowned.

"Wait a sec'! Paul Revere? I thought Ben Franklin and Thomas Edison did this stuff." But..., wanting to look brave in front of the others, he took his brother's hand. Kenneth grinned.

"See, guys? Earl's not getting electrocutionated, are you, brother?" Earl's grin was triumphant, but his eyebrows knotted together for a moment.

"This has got to be some kind of a trick."

"Vee need another volunteer for zee electro test!" said Kenneth. "Red..., grab hold of Earl's hand." Red touched Earl.

"Okay..., but this better not be a trick." He held on. Once Red had a firm grip, Kenneth slid the rod tip into the metal part of the socket for a split second, then slid it away. Electricity shot through him. It tickled its way though Earl.

Hair straight up, the wild-eyed victim..., ungrounded at the end of the line, about jumped out of his skin.

Earl felt Red trying to remove his hand, but it was as if they were glued together. His hand tingled and his nose twitched.

"Whoa! This is really weird!"

Red howled..., an eerie, high-pitched howl.

45

"Yeeaaowww!" He hugged himself and hopped about.
"Kenny, you rat!"

"Ohh, man! That was so neat!" said Earl. He looked at Kenneth. "How'dja do it?" Kenneth grinned like a Cheshire.

"Shh! Eees very beeeg secret!"

About that time, Pa came down, faced them, and rubbed his chin as his eyes adjusted to the dimness. Kenneth turned.

"Hey..., Pa!"

The rest chorused, "Hi, Pa," except for the neighbors who said, "Hello, Mister Benson." John Henry eyed his boys.

"Lights are flickering.... What are you up to?" From nowhere, Kenneth produced the bulb. The fishing rod had disappeared, and he had the most innocent look on his face as he faced his father.

"I was just showing the boys here the right and wrong way to change a lightbulb if one burns out, you know, so they won't go and get themselves electrocuted." Mister Benson's face pinched up, as if had a problem digesting this.

"No, I don't know. Whatever you're doing, give it up before you blow out the fuse box or start a fire." He turned, went back upstairs, closed the door and..., much to everyone's delight, Kenneth was right back at it again.

"Okay, gentlemens! Now I show you magic vith zee lightning bulba!" He wrapped the bulb in his handkerchief.

"You zee, gentlemens? It eees magic!" He smashed it against a support beam, opened the cloth, and showed the broken pieces to all. Everyone gawked, oohed, and ahhed, then stared in horror, as Kenneth ate the pieces..., all of them.

Earl shivered. The thought of needle-sharp glass and metal in Kenneth's mouth, throat, and stomach was a bit much. It reminded him of the day, last winter, when Ernie had stuck his tongue on the railroad track and it had frozen to the steel rail....

Lord knows what made Ernie do such a crazy thing. He just did.... and, then..., couldn't get it unstuck.

Earl's mind wandered back to that day....

"Ma ongue's uck! Ahoww! Helkh! Ahoww! Ih ah ain ahmun?" It was difficult to make out what Ernie said. Red knelt down to get a good, close look at the situation.

"Jeepers...! You are stuck, brother!" Brows knitted, he glanced up at Earl and Johnny. Ernie sobbed.

"Ahhowww!" He was beginning to panic, and Earl.... was wishing he hadn't told him so many spook stories lately. One tall tale in particular was about a lonesome, heartbroken old hobo getting run over by a train after his foot caught in the tracks. Earl had delightedly described, in great, gory detail, about how the man's body was torn into so many pieces. Then, late at night, if you watched the spot where he died, you saw parts floating in the air, trying to reconnect and put his bloody, mangled body back together. The story got better, scarier, after that, and Ernie.... had believed every word.

Now, here he was.... with his tongue glued to the track! Ernie sobbed up at Johnny and Earl.

"Ih ah ayne aminn?" Earl peered up and down the track.

Dang! He'll lose it if we don't do something! He knelt.

"No, Ernie..., the train ain't coming..., yet." Mind filled with guilt and fear. Dang it! Why'd I have to say yet? Why'd I have to go and tell him that stupid story? Johnny looked down at his brothers.

"Want me to go for help? I can run fast as anyone." A train whistle sounded in the distance. Red peered up the track.

"No time for that!" He pulled out his knife, hiding it from Ernie's eyes, but Johnny and Earl saw it..., and shrieked.

"No...! Don't cut his tongue off!"

Up, and off the track, Ernie left blood and bits of tissue

on the rail. He shrieked in agony. Earl sensed the taste of blood in his own mouth, and winced. Red snatched a handkerchief from a rear pocket and stuffed it into Ernie's mouth. Their brother's loud wails were muffled..., but only somewhat.

Red-faced, bawling like a newborn calf, Ernie had to be piggybacked. He was hurting, but at least he wasn't as scared..., now that he was no longer attached to the track. One more thing learned the hard way.

Headed home, Earl asked Red, "Were you really going to cut his tongue off?" The train whistle sounded, much louder, as they stepped onto the sidewalk at Plainville Avenue. Ernie squeezed Red's neck, and buried his wet face between his brother's broad shoulder blades to hide from the oncoming beast. Red stopped..., pried Ernie's fingers loose, then hoisted him farther up onto his back.

"No..., I was gonna try to slide the dull side of the blade between his tongue and the rail.... Didn't know what else to do."

Do as I say, not as I do. As Kenneth continued to eat the lightbulb, Earl's mind slid to another time when a lesson was learned by watching what his brother went through.... the time Kenneth had gotten drunk, playing his fiddle to earn drinks and money at a local bar....

He came home, got into an argument out in the garage with a friend over a girl, the disagreement escalated, and Kenneth smashed his fiddle over the guy's head.

The violin had broken into a thousand pieces, least that's what it looked like to Earl when he saw it the next morning.

Sobered up, Kenneth saw it, gave himself a thorough tongue-lashing, ran to the house, grabbed a broom, and headed back to the garage. Earl stood to one side as his brother swept the floor, swore at himself, and gathered fragments.

As Earl watched, Kenneth went to Pa's workbench, and

began putting pieces together. Not daring to speak, Earl hovered, nose wrinkling at the smell of the glue.

When things were shaping up, he said, "Gee, Kenny, you sure have lots of patience! Think you can fix it like it was?"

Kenneth continued working, but shortly said, "Brother, you never know if something will work unless you give it a try."

Days later, Earl looked in the garage. Kenneth's back was to the door. He was tuning the violin. Waxing and polishing finished, it shone in the dim light. Kenneth turned, then grinned.

"Done!" Earl turned as Red ran toward the house.

"Red! It's done! Kenny's ready to try it!" Red whooped and ran inside.

"Hey, everybody! Come on! Kenny's playing!"

Everyone crowded into the garage. Anticipation radiated from the whole family as Kenneth waited for them to settle. He rosined the bow, so it wouldn't slip on the strings, then cradled the violin beneath his chin.

"Well, here goes. Keep them fingers crossed." He pushed and pulled the old horsehair bow across the strings a few times, listening, to see if they'd held the stress of tuning and were still wound tight on the pegs. A smile crept over his lips. With long, confident strokes, he gave the instrument a full-fledged workout.

"Yee haw!" He grinned, and tapped his foot. "Ahh, yes! All right!" He did a little jig, and smiled broadly as everyone danced about. The fiddle... had never sounded better.

Kenneth found the sound exquisite, as did people who heard him play. No one could tell it had almost been destroyed forever. When offered a thousand dollars, Kenneth refused to sell. He would never part with his violin.

He's right, Earl decided, about not knowing if something

will work unless you try it.

Even if Kenneth was a corker, Earl learned quite a few things from him. The cork had managed to rub off onto all of the younger brothers.

Earl snapped out of his reverie..., then shuddered as Kenneth patted his lips with the edge of the empty handkerchief.

Kenny's eaten lightbulbs before; he'll probably do it again. He's a Benson and that's just the way it is.

Earl Benson 1934

CHAPTER
SIX

SNAKES, SKUNKS, AND OLD MISTER MOSES

The Benson brothers fished brooks that ran through land owned by Mister Moses. They contained nice speckled trout, which they caught even during droughts when creek beds were nothing but puddles. Walking in, pants rolled, they reached, barehanded, under rocks, grabbed fish, then slid them, through the gills, onto birch crotches shaped like wishbones.

One day, Earl figured he had a good-sized trout, but..., hauled it out, and found himself facing a big, black, slithering snake. Letting out a yelp that might have been heard in the next county, he threw the creature as far as strength allowed, then took off in the opposite direction.

"Yeeaoww! Sss-snake!" He fell against the creek bank, skinned both knees, and let out another yelp.

Everyone laughed. Earl glared. Red helped him up.

"Pete's sake, Earl! You're hopeless! It's just a little water snake." Earl felt his face grow hot. He eyed the area to make sure the snake was gone.

"Oh, yeah? You grab one, and see how you feel!" He brushed bloodied dirt off his knees. "Wasn't little, either, Mister Know-it-all-smarty-pants!"

Tommy Yabrosky smirked, then flicked a pebble at him.

"What'sa matter, Earl the pearl? Don't you like snakes?" Earl gave him his best drop dead look.

"No, and I don't have to! Bet there's things you don't like, either!"

Ernie ran over, wiped his nose on a dripping, wet sleeve and said, "Did he bite'cha, Earl? How big was he?" Earl reddened, still angry at himself for being a scaredy-cat, but..., calmer now that his heart had stopped trying to leap out of his chest. It all turned to panic again when Johnny hollered.

"Whoa! I see him! I'm keeping him for a pet!" He ran toward the snake, as it slithered behind a rock.

Hands on hips, Earl shouted, "You ain't keepin' no snake near me!" Johnny continued to look, anyway. Earl rolled thankful eyes toward heaven when Red put an end to the search, saying it was time to head home. Snakes gave Earl the Willies, and now.... he knew he'd never reach under another rock.

The boys had fair fishing gear, made of what they had, starting with a search of the woods for birch poles. At times, they'd saved to buy a tin trout reel that clicked when wound. Store-bought string or fishing line, if afforded, was put on the reel, which was tied to the pole with rope. Staples were pounded in along the rod. All together, it produced a good, limber pole, five or six feet long, that caught many fish.

More than once, out fishing, they saw a stranger, duded up in shiny new waders, machine stitched cotton vest, big fancy store bought pole, empty creel..., acting like he knew what it was all about. He hadn't caught any, so they sold him fish, getting ten cents each, which put a smile on his face and theirs' too.

"Bet he tells his wife all kinds of fish stories," said Earl as they headed home. Ma met them at the door.

"Any luck?"

"Nope. Weren't biting."

The boys felt the need for more money, and spent it on fish hooks and a few treats. Hustling made money each day and, most of it was given to Ma.... Everyone supported the family. She put earnings into the kitty..., meaning her pocketbook. If one made a dollar, she handed over a dime he, or she, could keep. The boys dashed to the store. Earl seldom thought about saving, and a favorite purchase was Mother Frisbie's coconut cream pie for ten cents.

Mister Benson managed the bowling alley and pool hall. The boys had night jobs, setting up pins, racking balls, mopping restrooms and cleaning. They caddied Saturdays, Sundays, or sometimes both days at the golf course at Avon, and often made double money by carrying two bags full of clubs at a time. After about the thirteenth hole, Earl was tired and anxious to be done.

One day, he caddied for Mister Goodyear, a good golfer, but, on this particular day, the man took a mighty swing, topped the ball, and it bounded down the fairway, then plopped into a big pond out on the back nine. He threw his club.

"Get in there and get my ball." He indicated the pond with an impatient nod. Earl eyed the water.

He's crazy! He frowned at Mister Goodyear.

"No way, sir!" The golfer threw his cap.

"Look here, Sonny!" he said, still pointing at the pond, "I paid damn good money for that ball. Now, go get it!" Earl stood firm.

"No, Sir! There's big snapping turtles and snakes in there. You can get it yourself if you want it that bad!" Goodyear gazed at the pond. He scratched his bare head for a few seconds.

"Snapping turtles and snakes, huh?" He looked at Earl, who nodded an affirmative, as Earl handed him his cap and iron.

"Awh, crap!" said Goodyear. He took out a new ball, and dropped it into the rough behind where the first ball had gone in. Earl watched as he readied, lined up the club head, concentrated on keeping his head down, and eyes on the ball.

The ball....flew low and to the right. Earl grimaced.

Nice backswing, but..., too fast, and his follow-through's rough. Water splashed as the ball sailed into a pond near the green. Earl turned away, darn near laughed out loud, twisted about, but found it impossible to keep a straight face.

Goodyear was not happy. As they approached the green, he did not ask.... if there were snapping turtles or snakes in this pond. He stopped..., stood with eyes closed..., then, after a few moments, opened them..., took another new ball from his bag..., dropped it on the ground..., and looked at Earl.

"Son..., this game will make you..., or break you. If you cheat..., you only hurt yourself..., and you do not learn self-discipline." He finished the last holes almost professionally, then surprised Earl with a fifty cent tip.

Earl loved the game, and learned by watching and listening to Mister Goodyear and other players. Sometimes, he got to keep old, unclaimed clubs that were lost on the course if the golf shop manager deemed them unsuitable for resale or renting out. Earl took as many as possible, and fixed them almost good as new. Thrilled with the unwanted clubs, he practiced golf shots at every opportunity, even after school started in the fall.

It was his opinion that old people were strange and..., yes, at times, very difficult to relate to.

Apparently feeling social obligation, or something of that nature, Ma, having discovered an ailing elderly widow, had arranged to have her boys take turns sitting with her at night.

Afraid to be alone, the lady must have appreciated the company, but he told Howard, "Jeepers, it's no wonder she's scared! Her house is creepy and dingy-dark. It's true, How! It smells all moldy like someone died in there..., a long time ago." Howard sighed, and rolled his eyes skyward.

54

"Grow up, Earl!" Red only added to Earl's fears.

"Yeah, I figure the old gal's got her husband's corpse hidden upstairs in a dark closet."

Earl hated each trip to the spooky, cobwebbed house. The oldness of the woman terrified him, but he put up a brave front, acting smooth and tough when his brothers teased about it. Then, his turn came to go sit with her. He tried everything, to get out of it, but..., ended up going anyway.

He knocked on her door.

"Shoot, she's almost old as Methuselah. She could die while I'm here." The idea of her kicking the bucket and falling flat on her face onto the cold, hardwood floor, right there in front of his eyes, mortified him. His palms were sweaty.

"What in God's name would I do?" He knocked again. Maybe she's dead already.... Guess I'll go ho...."

"Hello, Carl!" She opened the door and ushered him in, a delighted look on her face.

Later, she tottered out of her kitchen with a few powdered doughnuts stacked on a plate, as Earl twiddled his thumbs in his lap at the dining table.

Don't want to hurt her feelings, but..., maybe the old gal really has gone 'round the bend like Red said. Maybe she poisoned her husband. Maybe....

She waited, small, feeble..., hefty plateful of doughnuts in wrinkled, gray, ghostlike hands, an inocent, expectant smile etched upon her ancient face. Eyes covered by filmy off-white cataracts peered at him, and he wondered if, somehow, she saw just how intimidated and downright fearful he was of her. Taught politeness and respect for elders, he rose, pulled her chair out, and.... stared at the doughnuts. He sat down.

Poisoned..., or not? He cleared his throat.

"Those look pretty good."

"Please, help yourself, Carl," She wiped her hands on her stained apron. He blinked.

Man, I give up! She sure can't hear very well. Calls me Carl, no matter how many times I tell her I'm Earl. Sounds weak as a kitten, though, too frail and nice to hurt anyone. Guess I shouldn't believe that dumb stuff about her.... What the heck! If I die eating a doughnut..., I won't know the difference.

Taking the smallest of the powdery friedcakes from the plate, he remembered his manners.

"Thank you, Ma'am." He chanced a small bite as his hostess sat down. Stale and moldy. He nipped another bite from the doughnut, and smiled all too pleasantly when she peered over at him. Her hand came up to her mouth.

"Oh, dear! Now where have my manners gone off to, Carl? You need a big glass of milk to go with your snack." She tottered out to the kitchen.

Earl looked for an open window or convenient place to stash the doughnut. With no means of quick disposal, he jammed in a couple of huge bites, barely chewed, and nearly gagged, as he choked it down.

"Here you go, Carl." She set the glass on the table.

"Thanks," Earl mumbled through the mouthful. He washed the dry, musty mess down with a couple of gulps from the glass.

Least the milk's good. He sighed, then wiped his mouth and fingers on the white linen napkin she'd provided.

"Have another, Carl!" She pushed the plate closer. He noticed she still hadn't eaten one.

"Uh..., no thanks, ma'am, I ate too much at supper. You'd better put the rest away." He ducked his head, and stared down at his hands.

For the rest of the uncomfortable, long evening, he sat....

wondering if the doughnut was going to stay down and..., if it did, would it poison him? More important was whether or not this was the night she would die. He pictured her stiff corpse sprawled before him again. As the night wore on, she visited with him and, although he didn't contribute much conversation, he began to see her for what she was. He half-smiled.

She's just a lonely, scared old woman, all by herself. If I bring homework next time, I won't have to talk much. Still, I wish Ma would let me work at the bowling alley instead of this. Anything but this! God, please don't let me get old, and smell moldy-dead like her! Ma's words echoed through his head.

"Cleanliness is next to godliness. You don't have to be rich to be clean. Soap's cheap, and just 'cause your clothes ain't new doesn't mean they can't be clean!"

Later at home, he told himself, as he washed up for bed, "Well..., I guess Ma's right about that."

The old woman died. Earl and Red decided that her ghost had joined up with her husband's, and they were both wandering around that old place. Old people were scary.

Mister Moses.... was very scary.

One day, a bunch of boys sneaked over to his lumber mill when it was quiet and played outside in the steamy sawdust pile. Someone found an unlocked door, and everyone crept in to have a quick look around.

Ernie said, "Hey, you guys! We're not s'posed to be here. I wanna go home." He yanked Earl's sleeve.

"C'mon, Earl, let's go 'fore Old Man Moses gets us." Earl was too busy looking things over to respond. Twitching nostrils appreciated an interesting, aromatic assortment of oak, walnut, and cherry woods, combined with the heavy odor of well-oiled machinery. Donnie crept up behind him.

"Sure do like tools and machinery, don't you?" Earl was

about to answer, when Johnny gave Ernie a poke in the ribs.

"You're just chicken, so there! Brawwwk! Why don't you go out and play in the sawdust pile, chicken?"

Ernie poked Johnny back, and Johnny shoved his brother. Pushing his sleeve back, Ernie doubled up a fist.

"How'dju like a knuckle sandwich? You don't call me no chicken!" His bottom lip curled out and trembled. He stepped toward Johnny, then backed off. "I'm tired of playing in the sawdust, anyway." Earl pointed as he spoke.

"Good! Hand me that board over there." Johnny got to it first, and handed it over. Ernie pouted and glared.

"There's plenty of boards, Ernie," said Earl. "I need a bunch. If all you're gonna do is pout, I'll have to take you home and get the rooster to sit on your bottom lip." Ernie laughed.

"Roo would fall off..., 'cause he's too big!"

Johnny giggled, then added, "If you open your big mouth wide enough..., he'll fit just fine!"

Earl laid a rough-hewn board onto the rollers that carried huge tree trunks to the gigantic, round sawblade, climbed up, sat on the board, then said, "Okay, Donnie, give me a shove!" He rode the board all the way down the rollers until it bumped against the blade. He jumped off, added another board on top, then sent the two careening back down the rollers to Donnie. Each boy added to the stack when it was their turn, to see how many boards they could pile up and get all the way up or down the rollers. Ernie hunted up more boards from around the mill.

At this time, Lourden McKissick pulled a big handle back and forth that controlled huge double-pronged hooks that held logs in place on the rollers and pulled them toward the blade. He yanked until the prongs rested, unnoticed, against the saw blade. Earl's stack of twelve stopped at the end of the rollers.

"Beat that, Don!" He snapped his fingers, and whistled.

"Can't, can you?"

"Watch me," said Donald, adding another board to the tottering tower.

"Geronimo!" Thirteen boards sailed toward the blade.

"It's gonna fall!" yelled Johnny. The load wobbled, careening its wild way down the rollers.

"Hang on!" hollered Donnie. "You can make it!"

Everyone laughed and shouted. Right about then Lourden found an interesting button.... and..., pushed it.

The giant saw screamed into motion. Shark-like teeth on the huge spinning blade came into contact with steel prongs and stack of wood. The resulting explosion..., was of unimaginable proportion. Earl's hair stood on end as pieces of shattered wood and steel schrapnel whizzed by. Ear-piercing noise almost matched, in decibles and shrillness, the shrieking that came from himself and the others as they ducked and ran for the door.

Mister Moses tore out of his farmhouse, headed for the sawmill, shotgun loaded for bear.

"Ka-blam!" Earl didn't know what excuse he'd give Ma for his rock-salted backside this time, either. The boys stopped running only when well into the woods. Earl's chest heaved as he caught his breath.

"Man, did'ja see that? Stuff flying everywhere! Just like being in a real war!" Noticing Earl picking at the back of his britches, Johnny giggled.

"Man, are you gonna get it when we get home! Ma's gonna lick you with a willow switch, for sure!" Ernie gulped and wagged his head up and down. Earl frowned.

"You say nothing to no one about this. You hear? Besides..., if I get whooped, you might too." Johnny nodded.

"Yeah, gotta stick up for each other." Ernie wiped his nose on a sawdust-covered sleeve.

"Why don't you just tell Ma that Mister Moses was shooting at a crow, and you accidently got in the way?" Earl tugged a lock of Ernie's hair.

"Oh, yeah! Good one! Bet I beat all of you back to Webster Street!" They ran, and Earl let them win. Brothers were neat, sometimes, especially when they stood by you.

When the Benson boys stood up to someone, they fought fair, never seeking fights, but if anyone started it, they defended themselves and each other. If Earl fought a boy the same height and approximate build, and was beaten, Red or Howard picked him up, dusted him off, took him home, and gave him a boxing lesson, showing him fancy punches and defensive moves.

For awhile, Earl took a beating..., not just from the other boy, but from his brothers, too, until he learned defense. In the back of his mind was the thought that if he won he wouldn't get whomped by a brother. He had to win, was a quick study, and his brothers didn't hit hard. They roughhoused, enough to knock sense into and teach him. It was the same with Johnny and Ernie, only Earl helped teach them.

When a brother was beaten by a bigger bully, the next oldest beat the offender up. The Benson boys weren't picked on often. There were ruffians who thought themselves better, but the five brothers stuck together, defended each other, and knew right from wrong. Boxing was used only when necessary.

Earl enjoyed the challenge, and got to be good with his fists. A boxing ring, in the basement, was surrounded by ropes tied to support beams, and old mattresses were laid on the floor. When brothers argued, it was settled with boxing gloves. By the time a winner was announced, combatants were laughing so hard, neither remembered what the argument was about.

If things were to go right, one had to be responsible and decent, though difficult at times, and keep out of trouble. In a town the size of Unionville, one learned to get along, be polite, do good, go to church, not talk back to people, and be kind. Bad guys went to reform school. Earl felt he was a good guy, having never been in reform school, only the orphanage, and not because of anything he did or didn't do. At some point, he figured there was always someone around, here or there, to be accountable to..., except for Mister Moses, maybe.

October of 1934, Ma said, "You boys need to get a skunk, so I can render the fat for poultices for winter colds." Earl wanted a pelt to sell so that he'd have money to buy a red, white and blue yo-yo he'd seen at the five-and-dime store.

"You should see it, Dad! Colors spiral around, it has stars all over, it's so neat, and comes with instructions on how to do a hundred-and-one tricks!"

That evening, as he pulled on his jacket, Earl said, "Hurry it up, Ernie! Let's go get our skunk!" He picked up a flashlight and headed for the door. Pa came into the kitchen.

"Wait a minute, Earl. You remember everything I told you?" Earl answered from the back porch.

"Yup..., Don't try to kill it ourselves because we might miss, and the skunk will spray us." Ernie giggled.

"Yeah, Pa! We sure don't want that to happen!" Turning away, eyes twinkling, Pa poured himself a cup of coffee.

"That's right. Kenny or I will kill it after you get back, and leave the carcass out in the far corner of the lot until tomorrow. Whatever you do, don't let him get his feet on the ground or he'll wet his tail, and fling it at you." Earl laughed.

"No problem, Dad! We'll be back with it before you can whistle Yankee Doodle!" He pulled Ernie down the steps.

"C'mon, Poky!" Halfway across the yard, Ernie stopped.

"How do we catch the skunk?" Earl smiled.

"Nothing to it, Ernie. Catching 'em is simple. You do it

in the fall, when they're out looking for mates. You spot one, hold its attention by shining light in its eyes, that's your job, 'cause you're not even ten yet, then I sneak up..., and get him..., and that's it! Pa told me everything!"

"Oh..., that's easy...," said Ernie, as they climbed the fence. They crept across the field behind the house.

Didn't take long. Earl saw him first. The noisy, roving Romeo scratched and scent-marked the base of the big oak that stood near the middle of the field. Earl held a hand to his mouth and whispered into Ernie's ear.

"By the tree..., hold the light on him. Remember, jiggle it a little." Ernie jiggled to keep the skunk's wary attention while Earl circled around and crept up behind their prey.

"Gotcha! Ernie, I got him! Bring the light!" Growling, the skunk wriggled, trying to free itself, but Earl had a firm grip around the base of its tail.

"Hang on! I'm coming!" Ernie skampered toward him.

"Wow, he's big!" Ernie aimed the beam into the skunk's angry, jet-black eyes.

"Take the light out of his eyes! Oh, peeuww! Watch it! He's wetting all over! Gotta get home fast with this one. Man, oh, man! He's heavy! Shine the light! Head home, Ernie! Don't stop till you get there!" Earl held the struggling polecat way out in front of himself and walked behind his brother.

Halfway home, he said, "Pete's sake, Ernie, can'tcha go any faster? My arm's breaking! Hurry it up, wouldja?"

Ernie plodded along, increasing his pace. Earl glanced at him. Poky Ernie navigated the ruts in the field, shining the dim beam to light their way. The weight of the skunk, which Earl figured to be at least fifteen pounds, was unbearable. The skunk growled and struggled.

"Hold still, you dumb thing! Quit tha...!"

62

It slipped.

"Watch it! He got away...ayeee, my eyes!" Feet planted, the furious animal whipped its wet, scent-laden tail back and forth, spraying the air. Turning to see what was going on, Ernie flailed the air with his hands as spray hit him, and dropped the flashlight. It landed on the ground and illuminated the indignant skunk, which flipped its tail one last time, then disappeared across the dark field. The light... flickered, then died.

Eyes burning, Earl and Ernie could just about make each other out in the moonlight. They faced one another and began a furious fit of coughing, as tears streamed down their faces. Ernie let out a long wail.

"Stupid nincompoop! Now look what you done!"

"So...? Sorry! I couldn't hold him! What else you want me to say?" Earl kicked dirt toward where he thought Ernie was standing. Ernie was bawling. He coughed and sputtered.

"Wish I was big, so I could kick your stupid butt! I'd kick it all the way home!" He rammed a toe into the plowed up earth and sent it flying at his brother. "Stupid, stupid, dumb nincompoop!" Earl hands came up to protect himself.

"Shush your mouth, and get the flashlight! Can't stand out here arguing all night." Ernie stumbled over, found the flashlight, and groaned.

"Dang it, Earl! Why'd you have to go and drop him? Now look at us! Man, oh, man! Ma's gonna be spitting mad!"

Earl walked along a deep plowed furrow. Ernie caught up and grabbed onto his brother's shirttail.

"Peeeuww! You sure do stink!"

"Me?" said Earl. "And you think you don't? Hah! You smell worse than that old skunk ever did, knucklehead! Boy, Ernie! Sometimes you can be so dumb!"

When they crossed the fence and stumbled into the back

yard, the dog let out a howl. Ma came out on the back porch and was soon fit to be tied. Nostrils pinched, she started in, hollering and shaking her finger, which reminded Earl of the old folklore tale he had studied in school about a female spirit, a banshee, believed to wail outside a house as a warning that a death would occur soon in the family. He shuddered, then laid a protective hand on Ernie's shoulder.

"Sheesh! I feel bad enough without her carrying on. Sounds kinda funny though, with her nose pinched like that."

Pa stuck his head out to see what had the dog stirred up. His jaw dropped. "Didn't remember what I told you, did you?"

"But, Dad, Pa..., I... it...." Earl moved toward the porch.

"No!" screeched Ma. "Stay where you are!" She shook her finger until Earl was sure it would fall off. "Don't you dare come closer to this house!"

Soon, everyone was out there, noses pinched shut. There was lots of hollering back and forth that reminded Earl of the nasal-like honking of a gigantic, disgruntled gaggle of geese.

Ma took two washtubs and scrub brushes from the nails they hung on, and pitched them into the yard.

"Stay there! Don't move until I get some water heated." She ran into the house, slamming the door behind her, but Earl still heard her giving orders to his sisters, brothers and father.

When the water was hot, Ma said, "Get them clothes off and drop them by the back fence! Red, get the shovels! Kenny, help him dig a hole!" Earl and Ernie stood naked and shivering in the cool night air as they waited for orders. Ma sent buckets of water out to fill the tubs. Pa poured lots of soap flakes into each, then backed off as the boys walked over and climbed in. Kenneth and Red dug a hole and shoveled the boys' clothes in.

"Wheeuww!" said Red. He whistled shrilly and shoveled dirt back into the hole. "We'll never get rid of the smell!"

"Be all but gone in a week or two," said Kenneth. "Then these can be dug up and washed."

"Should just pitch them out in the woods," huffed Red.

"Can't afford that," said Kenneth, packing dirt down with the back of the shovel. They put the shovels away and retreated into the house. Ma hollered through the screen door.

"Don't come in here, now, until you've scrubbed every last inch of yourselves! How you boys manage to get yourselves into these predicaments, I'll never know!" Her voice was muffled when she closed the door.

"Ought to make both of you sleep out there with that mangy old dog tonight!"

Sitting out there in the dim porchlight, all by themselves, skins scrubbed bright pink, the boys found they couldn't look at each other without giggling. Part of this was because they were sculpting beards, mustaches, and fluffy, piled up hairdos out of the suds. Earl hooted with laughter and pointed at Ernie.

"Oh, man! Unbelievable! You look just like Ma!" They squealed with laughter. Ernie swirled another curl into his coiffure, scowled, then pointed an accusing finger at his brother.

"Yeeoou... stink!" Earl finished the exclamation.

"Like a skunk!" They struggled to keep straight faces and be quiet, but, just when Earl thought he had it under control, Ernie howled, then pinched his nose shut and did a perfect, twangy imitation of Ma.

He shook his finger, and mimicked, "I ought to make both of you sleep out there with that mangy old dog tonight!" They turned redder in the effort to contain themselves but, unable to do so, peals of laughter resounded across the yard and into the cool night air. Eyes full of tears, Earl gasped, then giggled.

"Oh, man! We gotta stop, or Ma will come out here!"

For a few seconds..., they were quiet. Only then.... could

they hear the snickering, hoots, and laughter that came from within the house.

Because the odor persisted, the boys not only dealt with incessant scolding from Ma, but new nicknames from Pa that hung on for days..., Smelly and Stinky. Earl shook his head.

"Least I'm Smelly! I guess my yo-yo's gonna have to wait. Ain't saying nothin' about it, neither..., 'cause I don't want anyone callin' me Smelly Yo-Yo!"

For Earl, Autumn was the most beautiful season, so spectacular were the leaves turning their magnificent colors. He loved to see and hear squirrels scampering across the crispy-dry, foliage-covered ground, in a hurried effort to bury acorns away for the coming winter. The smell of leaves burning in peoples' yards was something he savored. It was his favorite time of year and he especially liked Halloween.

Grouchy old Mister Moses hated Halloween. First off, he didn't need a costume because he was spindly-tall, and spooky looking, a scraggly old scarecrow with long gray hair and scrawny beard. Earl rarely got a close look, because he was always keeping his distance from the old man.

The Webster Street boys pulled tricks on Halloween. This year they had planned ahead. All summer, the boys had collected pieces of rope here and there.

When it was dusk, they sneaked onto Moses' property and waited, hidden, until he entered his outhouse. Someone had said he was only half deaf, so they had to distract him.

Two younger boys paraded up and down outside the fence with sticks that had rope loops attached to the ends. Laughing and carrying on, they twirled the lassos in plain sight, so Moses would watch through the cracks in the outhouse door.

"Yahoo! Ride, dumb cowboy!"

Back of the outhouse, Ernie whispered, "Dumb cowboy?"

Figuring the cowboys had Mister Moses' full attention, two boys climbed the walnut tree behind the outhouse. Earl stood with Donnie, under the tree. Johnny, Ernie, and a couple more of the gang joined them. Since Earl was the oldest below, he threw the rope to the boys in the tree, and it was caught on the first toss. A loop was made, the outhouse lassoed, and the boys dropped to the ground. Everyone grabbed the rope as the fence line cowboys continued their charade.

"Yahoo! Get back here, hoss! Gotta get the bad guys!"

A silent, "One..., two..., three...!" was mouthed. The rope tightened. With a loud creak and ominous groan, and Earl wasn't sure if the groan came from the shack..., or from Mister Moses..., the solid outhouse toppled over onto its door.

"Ka-blam!" The shotgun blast sent splinters and boys flying. Scattered in all directions, starting with straight up, they ran for the woods.

Even from way over there they saw and heard a good deal of purple smoke pandemonium coming from the privy. Moses was in there yelling a few really neat cusswords loud enough to be heard all over Unionville. The outhouse rocked; the old man was furious, stuck for sure, with only one way out.... through the hole in the bottom.

No one hated Halloween more than Mister Moses.

CHAPTER SEVEN

TILL SOMETHING BETTER COMES ALONG

In 1935, when Earl was twelve, many knitting mills and businesses closed. The country's shaky economy hit hard. Pa worked at Winstead's mill as things slowed at the Myrtle mill. One of the last laid off, he worked in Winstead as many hours as possible. When things picked up, he earned thirty-five dollars a week, but it had to support a family with seven children still at home. The money didn't buy enough, so he took odd jobs, and built Adirondack chairs he talked folks into buying. Earl loved watching him make things.

In September, at age thirteen, Earl decided girls were okay. School started, and he met his first girlfriend, brown-haired Sally. He walked her to their next class. Not much to look at, but she's nice! My girl! Least, I hope so. Friendly, but that's about it. Sally was interested in older boys, and Earl gave up.

In 1936, he met his first real girfriend, Jean, fourteen, good-looking, blonde, nicely shaped. Fourteen, he was head over heels in love, but there was a problem..., a huge problem. Jean's younger brother disliked boys hanging around her. Earl walked her home one day.

How do I tell her how I feel without messing up? I've gotta find a way! Near her home, they stopped on the corner. Quite confident, Earl managed the conversation well. Moving closer, though, his tongue tied a nice knot as he took her hand.

"I...., uh...,"

"Yeeeaaghh!" Huge arms encircled him. Arms pinned, engulfed in a suffocating bear hug, he was hoisted into the air. Earl suddenly felt great compassion for the skunk he'd sneaked up on three years ago. Unable to breathe, he struggled, trying to break away.

"Yeah! Gotcha, Squirrely Early! Earl's face was beet-red.

"Pudgy rat! Put me down," he said, as he was bounced up and down.

"Put him down!" yelled Jean, hands on hips.

"Uh, okay," said her brother. He grinned at her, opened his arms wide, and let go. Earl landed in a heap at her feet.

"Geeee whiz, you're no fun." He lumbered away. As 'Squeezer' headed up the street, Earl heard him laugh. Too flustered to say much, let alone attempt to tell her of his undying love, Earl told Jean he had to go.

Several times, about to reveal his feelings, he fell victim.

"I've got to stop letting him get away with his stupid games. Big lout's gonna kill me! Should've taken the bird turd down a peg or two the first time, but I didn't want Jean upset."

Walking her home one day, he said, "I've lost it with your brother. He's had a chance. Won't hurt him bad, but I'm not taking anymore." They stopped beneath a towering oak, up the street from her home. His stomach fluttered like the last few leaves of autumn floating down to kiss the ground at their feet.

Jean picked one up. "So beautiful and perfect!" she whispered, turning it over in her hands. "I love shades of red. Guess that's why I like your hair so much. Wish mine was like yours." Earl faced her, heart tap dancing in his throat, took the leaf and gave it a slow turn, as he gazed at it. The smell of leaves burning somewhere up the street was acrid-sweet and intoxicating.

"It is a beauty," he said softly. "Couldn't ask for anything to be more perfect." He gazed at her. So beautiful..., so perfect..., like her. He stared into her eyes.

I'm winning her over. God, please, give me the right words to say! Jean moved closer and held out her hand. He took it gently into his and, remembering a story about a gallant knight kissing a fair maiden's hand, bent to tenderly kiss the back of his fair lady Jean's delicate, ha....

"Eeeeyaaahh! Once again, he was trapped by the plump-as-a-dumpling arms of unrelenting Squeezer. This wasn't what he'd planned and, this time, he regretted the torment he himself had dished out to his own sisters' boyfriends. Again, breath was squeezed from his burning lungs, but he was ready, and thoroughly angered at losing the chance to endear himself into Jean's heart. His hard-heeled boots kicked against the aggressor's shins and knees. Simultaneously, he relaxed, sank into himself and wiggled downward enough to free an arm.

"Oomph," grunted Squeezer, as Earl elbowed him in the stomach. He loosened his grip just enough. Earl broke away, then spun about to face his assailant.

"Warned you, ya stupid idiot!" He nailed Squeezer in the stomach with a hard fist.

Nothing happened. He hit again, hard as he could, but it didn't phase the oversized, dough-bellied boy, who kept laughing, but, then..., Earl jumped up, and smashed a hard fist into his nose.

"Now laugh, you dumb hyena!"

Wide-eyed, hand clapped over open mouth, Jean was frozen in place. Blood rolled down across her brother's lips onto his hands, which he'd brought up to protect himself from another blow. Astonishment was plastered across his overfed face. Earl leaned against the trunk of the old oak, gasping for

71

breath, as Squeezer sputtered, spit blood, then spoke through cupped hands.

"You bwoke mah nose!" Earl's look at Jean was apologetic. Then, he scowled at her brother.

"If I broke it, you deserved it, dummy. Just 'cause you're big, doesn't mean you can get away with being a bully."

"Oh yeah..., Well, I'm telling!" Squeezer stormed off, blubbering, then clomped up the steps of the house.

"Mama! I been beat up by one of the Benson boys!" The screen door banged. Earl straightened, walked over to Jean, then took her hand.

"Sorry..., he pushed it too far." He peered into her eyes, seeking forgiveness, or something, but saw only bewildered confusion. He bit down on his lower lip.

Great! Haven't got to first base, and now she's upset with me. I've lost her for sure! Jean looked into his eyes.

"I'm sorry, too. When my parents hear about this they'll hate you. I can't let you walk me home anymore. It's just not going to work, but we can see each other at school and maybe meet somewhere Saturday, if you're not busy." She kissed Earl on the cheek, a soft kiss, so close to his lips, he was stunned.

Holy moly! I gotta tell her how I feel! He opened his mouth, then closed it as the screen door opened.

"Uh oh!" said Jean. Mrs. Squeezer stormed down the porch steps, then up the street, and..., she was screaming like a banshee. Earl stiffened.

"Whoa, sounds bad as Ma! Guess I'm not welcome around here anymore." He squeezed Jean's hand. She held tight for a moment, then let go.

"G'bye," she whispered. "See you at school." He walked up the street. Jean's mother thundered over to where she stood. Earl glanced back, and saw his beautiful Jean gazing back. Her incensed, overprotective mother was screeching.

"You better be going! You've got some nerve, beating up my little boy! We will not have your kind of riffraff trash causing trouble in the neighborhood for us decent people! You get yourself on out of here and don't you let me catch you around here again! Not ever! Do you hear me?"

Except for a few very well planned, uneventful meetings between them, that was the end of the relationship.

During the spring of 1937, when Earl was still fourteen and his father sixty, Pa constructed a hot dog cart. He had a good business going on the sidewalks of downtown Unionville, and made up a song he sang to attract customers. His ability to stay on key and put so much emphasis into what he sang, amazed Earl, who smiled as he watched. The smell of sizzling hot dogs filled the air.

"I've got 'em all ready and I've got 'em all hot," sang John Henry as he gazed happily at the world through wire-rimmed spectacles. Blue eyes sparkled with warmth, satisfaction, and pride, beneath the wide brim of the soft hat covering his thinning white hair. Contentment radiated from him whether he made a sale or not. Long-sleeved shirt and slightly rumpled trousers covered his not-too-thin body. His white apron was stained here and there with condiments. For being so quiet around the house, he had a surprisingly strong, well-seasoned voice.

"Put the doggie in the middle and the mustard on top!" Earl was proud, though a bit abashed, at his father's boldness.

That takes guts. Wonder if I'll ever be as good with people as he is? Earl moved closer.

"You know, Dad, I want to be like you when I'm older. Everyone likes you a lot, and it's neat, how you talk and visit with them. I wish I had your courage and personality, but I

hope I have a better paying job than this when I'm your age."
Somehow, that last part didn't come out quite right. John Henry
laughed, and patted Earl's back.

"Son, you do what you have to..., to get by in this old
world, always doing your best, and doing what you can to
improve your situation. If it means selling hot dogs on some
street corner until something better comes along, then that's
what you do. Don't tell your ma, but, I'm saving for a down
payment on the building across from the bowling alley. I'm
opening a diner, and I guarantee I'll have a great business."

When the school year ended, Earl began working full time
to help support the family.

In the fall of 1937, Mister Benson returned to work at
Myrtle Knitting Mill. Earl dropped out of school and got a job
there, making fifteen dollars and sixty-one cents for a forty hour
week. Ma took his first check and gave him a dollar.

"This is ridiculous!" he told Red. "I need more money,
now I'm older. Here I am, running around with a couple of nice
girls, and broke all the time. I don't have much time, but at least
I could take them to movies or get ice cream cones and walk
around downtown. I don't need lots to spend on them, just
enough to impress them."

Next paycheck in hand, he summoned courage, and spoke
to Ma, deciding not to mention girls as he covered the subject.

"I need a pair of work boots to wear at the mill." He
halfways expected her response.

"Start saving your allowance or, better yet, get a pair at
the secondhand store. You're not getting more money. You'll
give me your check and take your allowance, or else!" He
didn't bother to ask what "or else" meant as he gave it up. She
went into her purse, dug into its depths, brought out a wrinkled
dollar bill, and handed it over. He stared at it, then at her. Heat

rose up his neck and face.

"One dollar? Out of the twelve, almost thirteen dollars I made after taxes, that's insane!" Her look was matter-of-fact.

"That is your allotment for the week."

Hands extended, palms up, he said, "Ma, I gotta get a pair of jeans so I'll have something decent to wear for..." He didn't get a chance to finish.

"You have jeans! I sorted two pairs from the wash that Red outgrew. They're in your drawer, if you'll bother to look, young man!" He thumped the doorjamb with the toe of his boot.

She can't even call me by my name!

"Yeah..., and they're patched and full of holes! I can't wear holy jeans to go...." Again he was interrupted by his mother, who snapped and unsnapped her coin purse.

"You know the rules! Whether you choose to follow them, or not, is completely up to you!" She snapped the purse shut and dropped it in her bag. Earl put his hands on his hips.

I can't believe her tightwadded stubbornness! I am not giving up. I'm at the end of my rope with her.

"Hold on a minute! This ain't gonna work! Pete's sake, Ma! I'm older now. I need more money, and I'm not giving you my whole check!" Clutching purse in one hand and briskly sweeping the fingers of the other through freshly salon-styled blonde curls, his mother glared through sharp, crystal-blue eyes.

"Young man, don't even begin to try to give me any of your ridiculous song and dance! You will give me your checks to help support this house, or out you go!" Glaring, seething, teeth clenched so hard his jaw ached..., he knew to back down.

"The heck with this!" he muttered, stomping out of the house. The door slammed. He stormed up the street.

Ain't letting her do this to me anymore. Somehow, I gotta get enough money to get out on my own.

Working in the mill was a well-paying, but dangerous job. One had to be careful around the equipment. As a bobbin boy, Earl discovered he had to watch every step to avoid being run over or crushed. The mill consisted of big open floors full of massive machinery, with one cubbyhole latrine on each story. Back-to-back, bobbin machines ran on tracks.

The process of spinning yarn started with several tall spools of soft dyed cotton or wool fiber that could be pulled apart like a cotton puff. Seeing and touching it reminded Earl of the colorful cotton candy he'd had once at a carnival. He loved the array of colors that were brought up and loaded onto steel posts of several huge stationary platform machines. Fiber from each spool was unwound enough to reach over to and be attached to empty bobbins that sat on posts of several receiving bobbin machines.

Bobbin machines faced the platforms and rolled out on tracks just so far, stretching fibers coming off large spools. Several strands unrolled from each spool as the spinning machine moved outward. After reaching the end of the track, the machinery went into motion, causing the fibers to jump up and down and rotate. Twisting and bouncing produced usable yarn which was wound onto the bobbins when the machine rolled toward the platform again. The process repeated until a bobbin cone was full or a feeding spool empty.

Mister Benson tended the loading of spools. When strands parted, they were rejoined with a quick twist of his fingers. It was Earl's responsibility to remove full bobbins and load new, empty cones onto the posts. When a cart was full of colorful, finished bobbins, he took them downstairs where they were knitted into beautiful sweaters and blankets.

Smoking wasn't allowed, with fibers floating about. Most men chewed tobacco and spit on the wood floor. Grease and oil coated the floor, too, making it slick. During the first two months, Earl didn't smoke on breaks for fear of being seen. As far as he knew, Pa was unaware of the habit, and he wanted to keep it that way. His refuge was the latrine, when available. He'd smoke half a cigarette, snub it out, and save the rest.

One day, during break, Pa approached, took out a plug of tobacco, cut a hefty piece, then held it between thumb and knife blade. A few men stood near, chewing and spitting. John Henry almost put it into his mouth, but hesitated. Blue eyes twinkled; a subtle smile crossed his lips. Indicating the tobacco with a nod, he held it out to Earl.

"Son, since you can't smoke, would you like a chaw of applejack?" Earl stared at it.

I'll be dipped. Pa knows. He's gonna treat me like one of the guys! He took a deep breath.

"Uh, sure, Dad. I'll try it. Thanks!" He took the plug and tucked it behind his lower lip. The big chunk made it impossible to keep his lips together as he worked it. He nodded, half-grinned at Pa and the men, then spat a dark stream of juice at the floor as if he'd done it a hundred times. Pa frowned.

"Don't be a hotshot, Son. There's always something or someone around that'll knock you off your high horse quicker than you can blink. Time's wasting. Let's get back to work!" Earl fought to keep the tarry mess from dribbling down his chin.

Not a cigarette, but it'll do. He thought of spitting out the big wad, but noticed men watching, as if waiting for him to do just that. He caught a glimpse of green passed between two.

Well, I'll be hanged..., they're betting on me. Wonder which way Pa's going with this? Well, if it's a show they want, they'll get one. In the next few minutes, he chewed and spat.

That'll show them! Working full-out, he soon had a cart to take down. He strutted, pushing it to the freight elevator.

"Hey, Bobbin boy! Tell them nitwits down there to weave you into their next blanket!" One had to yell to be heard. Earl turned, raised up, opened his mouth, to answer and, in one split second, slipped on the slime, fell on his butt, and swallowed the plug. He sat, dumbstruck, face crimsom, as men gathered, laughed, and slapped their knees. Then, Pa joined in.

"Awwh, go take a spin on a bobbin post!" Earl choked out. This remark brought more hoots and laughter with most of the men bent double. The effects of the tobacco, made his ears ring. Loud guffaws fuzzed together with buzzing in his head. Vision blurred, then cleared a bit, as he forced himself to concentrate on a dark spot of oil on the floor.

It hit. Wave after wave of sea-slimy-green, overwhelming nausea, that churned and grew as he sat on the cold, well-oiled, saliva-slick floor. Elbows pressed hard against sides, hands clutched about his stomach, he scrambled to his feet. The floor wavered.

"Whoa, Son! You don't look so good." Pa frowned at the men. "Let's get back to work." The crowd left them alone.

"I'm sorry," Pa began. He reached toward his son.

"I'm gonna be sick," Earl mumbled. He half-ran, stumbling toward the far-off latrine, and was relieved to find it empty. It felt as if he was turned inside-out as he lost chaw, breakfast, and the desire to ever chew again.

As he left the latrine, he tried to lose the proud image of himself riding a tall horse through the mill as everyone bowed and saluted. He shook his head.

"Oh..., man! Where did that come from?"

CHAPTER EIGHT

YOU'RE OUT

February, 1938, Earl had his paycheck from the mill.

"It's not fair. I'm right, doggone it, and she's wrong!"
He cashed it, headed for home, then steeled himself as he
walked in. Ma faced him, hand out, as he entered the kitchen.

"Give me your check." Stomach churned as it headed for
his throat. Confidence abandoned him.

Gotta stand up to her. He swallowed hard.

"I already cashed it, but here's my rent money." He
produced a crisp ten dollar bill. Ma moved toward him. A chill,
cold as ice, filled with fear, swept the length of his spine.
Snatching the bill, she glared at him.

"This ain't gonna work. You know the rules. Now,
where's the rest?" Angry fingers swept over his empty shirt
pocket. He stepped back as she reached for his pants pocket.

"Come on. Out with it!" Earl brushed her hand away.

"I've only got two dollars and some change left!"

"Well, that's two dollars and some change too much.
Hand it over, young man! Who told you to cash it, anyway?"

"I cashed it, and I didn't need anyone to tell me to do it,
either!" He felt himself shaking.

Why am I so damned afraid of her? Anger and frustration
swept though him.

"You've gotten all you're getting, Ma! Forty dollars a
month is more than enough!"

She strode to the stove, picked up a cooking fork, turned,

and waved it at him.

"Young man, you know I need that money to support this house. You're damn lucky I give you an allowance!"

"That does it!" Earl swore.

"Support the house? You're crazy! You mean support yourself, don't you, Ma?" It was too late to take it back..., what he'd said was true. He didn't want to take it back. Not now..., not ever. Her mouth fell open. She sputtered.

"Get out of my house..., right now!" She flung the back door open. It crashed against the wall.

"Get out, you ungrateful little bastard!" Earl moved toward the door, then turned, and looked hard into her eyes.

"By the way, Ma..., my name is Earl! E-A-R-L! Not young man! Not bastard..., 'cause that.... would make you look pretty bad, now, wouldn't it?" He stormed out, and slammed the door. "My name is Earl!" Her screeching followed him from inside the house as he goose-stepped down the driveway.

"Heil Hitler, you old biddy!" He tore, hell-bent, up the street. She flung the front door open.

"Get back here and give me that money, young man!"

Downtown, he spent some of the hard-earned cash, then came home sometime between nine and ten. The house was dark. Halfway up the snow-covered back steps, he stopped.

"Awh, crap...!" An old suitcase and items of his clothing, were strewn across the porch. The light came on, the back door opened a crack, and Ma's voice came at him.

"Well..., look who's here.... It is.... EARL..., isn't it? E-A-R-L? Well, you're out, Earl, and don't you ever come back!" She closed the door, he heard the key turn..., and the light went out, leaving him in darkness, glaring at the door. He picked up his things, stuffed them into the suitcase, made a nasty remark under his breath, then snapped it shut.

80

"Heil Hitler!" He stiff-fingered the door, turned, stomped down the steps, stormed toward the front of the house, then banged his fist along the siding.

"Hope your hair falls out, Ma! Dad, you better leave the old witch while you still can!" The front door swung open.

"Get out of here, or I'll have you arrested!"

There he was, trudging along, suitcase in hand, downtown Unionville, Connecticut, big town, where they rolled the sidewalks up at eight o'clock every night, nowhere to go, things looking dismal. He had a dollar and some change left.

"Thanks a lot, Ma!" He trudged along with no idea of where he was headed.

"Now what the devil am I gonna do?" Snow fell, softly at first, then harder. He plodded along on the dim-lit, empty street.

"Of all the times to shoot my mouth off..., I had to do it when a blizzard hit!"

From out of nowhere, Howard skidded, and bumped into his backside. Earl paused, then faced him. Howard frowned.

"What on earth are you doing hanging around here with a suitcase?" They stepped along the snow-covered walk.

"Well, brother..., our beloved mother just threw me out." Howard stopped, clutched his hands over his heart, and leaned against a lamp pole.

"No...! Not our dear, sainted mother! She wouldn't do such a terrible thing!" He was chewing and Earl watched, half amused, as he spun around the pole and spat into the street.

"Oh..., but she did." Earl set the suitcase down then straddled it. The steel snaps felt cold through the seat of his patched overalls. He looked hard at his brother, then got up and reached into his coat pocket for a cigarette. Hands shaking, he struck a match against the pole, lit up, then inhaled deeply.

Howard scratched his head for a long moment.

"So..., Ma threw you out, huh? Well, brother, what're you going to do?" Head bowed, Earl thrust the toe of his boot against the slickness of the sidewalk. Desperate eyes met older, concerned ones. He tried to keep his voice steady.

"I don't know, Howie. I just..., I don't have much money, so God knows what I'm going to find to rent." Howard spat another stream of tobacco juice into the street.

"Well..., you can't sleep in the park, ya know..., I tried that when she threw me out..., damn-near froze to death." He sighed, as if he knew what Earl was feeling, then spoke again.

"Awh, shoot..., you can't stand around here all night with your bare face hanging out. I got my trailer, so how'd you like to come stay with me till you get on your feet?" Earl nodded.

"Won't be long, How..., I'm making good money. Man, it's cold!" Snow bit at their faces, and Earl's fingers were numb as they made their way up the street. Howard took the suitcase in one hand and patted Earl on the back with the other.

"Proud of you, brother. Took guts to stand up to her." Earl smiled over at him.

"Once again, Howie..., you're my to-the-rescue, real live hero. Maybe things aren't so bad after all."

It was at least a month before Earl spoke to Ma or ventured into her house. She had little to do with him and less to say unless he fixed things around the place or did her a favor.

Howard left Unionville five months after Earl had moved in with him. He joined the Civilian Conservation Corps and traveled to Golden and Morrison, Colorado, west of Denver. He helped build roads there, and sent a couple of beautiful postcards home.

Wednesday afternoon, September 21'st, 1938, as Earl

walked along the sidewalk in downtown Unionville, the sky was slate-colored, filled with dark gray, yellow-edged clouds. The wind picked up. Rain, sand, and leaves stung his hands and face. He leaned against the gale.

"Whoa! What's going on? I've never seen anything like this! Gotta get home!" Not knowing why, he pushed on.

"Best take the shortcut through the woods." He ducked between two buildings, then crossed the freight yard, but, as he neared the tracks, the wind howled. A huge sheet of tin rolled toward him. He stepped behind a pole as it whipped by. He fought his way across the tracks, then up onto the sidewalk. Glancing back, he saw a power line snap, as the pole toppled. Sparks lit up everywhere as the line was blown against the roof and side of the freight storage building he had just come by.

"Run...!" cried a voice in his head. Wind and rain pounded legs and body. It felt as if he was fighting the current of a swollen river as he made his way into the woods. Here, trees blocked the full impact of the howling storm. As he stepped over fallen limbs, the voice propelled him.

"Run home...." He slipped through a fence bordering one of Mister Moses' fields. Mud sucked at his shoes. Wind ripped at his clothing. Air permeated with water, leaves, and debris made each breath a challenge.

"Run..., run home! He reached the fence bordering the back of his father's property, and heard loud snapping and cracking as a huge tree crashed onto the garage.

Then..., he was on the back porch, back to the door, sweeping a wet hand across his face and through his hair.

"What on earth made me come here? Trailer would've been a lot closer!" He'd fought to get here. Why? The door opened, hands grabbed him, and he was yanked backwards.

"Get in here, ya damn fool! You'll be blown away out

there!" Ma yelled. In the kitchen, she threw a towel at him.

"Tomorrow, get your belongings, if they're still there, then get yourself back here. You can give me ten dollars a week rent, and keep the rest of your check.

The next day, Earl checked the trailer. It'd been rolled and smashed. He salvaged what he could, then went home.

Late April of 1939 was putting buds on the hazelnut shrubs that lined the embankment along the driveway, opposite the house. New leaves unfolded on trees. Earl stared at the cards Howard had sent. Their picturesque scenery made him envious of his brother's situation, and the idea of traveling to a far away place was intriguing. The C.C.C. paid thirty dollars a month, which sounded fine because they also provided meals, clothing, free medical and dental care, and a place to sleep.

Sixteen, anxious for his own exciting adventure, he joined, following in Howard's footsteps, then bragged to anyone who'd listen that he was going to travel, just like Howie.

"Yeah..., I'm seeing all the places he wrote about, and it'll be great!"

Instead, he worked near home, in Connecticut and Massachussets, clearing roads, rebuilding bridges, and cleaning up extensive amounts of debris scattered about by the monster hurricane that had dealt the Atlantic coastline a terrible, crushing blow in September. The same storm had downed the tree that had torn into the garage. About to turn seventeen, he was appointed barracks leader. The position was a challenge, with thirty-five to forty rough-and-ready young men under his supervision, many bigger than himself. He managed each situation as it came and, after a six-month stint, was exhausted and homesick.

He went home.   Howard was back, making good money

working for A.G. Butler, whose trucking company was based in Collinsville. Positions were available in West Hartford and Farmington.

In July of 1940, Earl asked Howard if he'd put in a good word for him so he could get a job there too. At the end of the month, he was hired to haul trap rock to Windsor Locks where they were building runways for the airbase.

Late August, 1941, after working for Butler for just over a year, Earl was driving a fully loaded dumptruck to Unionville. He spotted Bobby Pelletier alongside the road, arm outstretched, thumb extended, and pulled over. Bobby ran up, waving.

"Hey, Earl! I gotta catch a lift into town. Can I ride with you?" Earl tapped the top of the steering wheel.

"Bobby, ole buddy, you know the rules. It's illegal to let minors ride." Bobby looked at him.

"Come on! I wouldn't be asking if it wasn't important! Let me ride, just this once. Please?" Earl looked skyward.

"Okay..., but hurry, and keep down, so nobody sees you." Bobby climbed in. Earl checked his rearviews, then pulled onto the road. Bobby grinned, then began to talk his ear off.

Driving along, absorbed in conversation, Earl was looking at him when the driver of a car, two cars ahead, slammed on his brakes to turn into a driveway. The elderly man in the car ahead of the truck, jammed on his brakes to keep from running into the turning car. Earl looked in the nick of time.

"Son-of-a...!" He stomped the brake pedal. No way to stop in time. Turning the wheel, he forced the truck hard to the right, missed the car, then swore as the truck headed up a steep embankment..., as if it had developed a mind entirely its own! It bounced and bumped, then, finally..., stopped.

Wide-eyed, screaming, holding on for dear life, Bobby suddenly shut his mouth and eyed Earl with obvious relief.

It was deathly quiet..., seemed, for a moment, as if they'd stay put..., then the worst thing that could have happened, did. The massive truck shuddered..., then toppled ponderously over onto its side like an elephant rolling onto its enormous flank during a circus act. It landed on the driver's side with a sickening thud, pinning Earl's door against the pavement.

Wide-eyed, screaming, Bobby landed atop Earl, who barely heard him. The load of rock spilling onto the road sounded like a million giant, clattering marbles dropped by a careless child from atop New York's Empire State Building.

Earl untangled himself from Bobby and, realizing neither was hurt, pushed against his friend's backside.

"Come on! Move! Get out, or I'll really be in trouble!" He shoved Bobby up through the passenger side window.

"Beat it, before they see you!" Bobby topped the embankment and ran into the woods as Earl got out of the cab.

Staring, dumbstruck at the catastrophe before him, he slapped his forehead, then found his voice.

"Unbelievable! Whole damn load of rock all over both lanes, and the stupid truck on its side!" Dismayed, sweating, swearing at no one in particular, he peered up the road.

"Never saw it! Old geezer must not of heard it either. Dang ole guy didn't even bother to check his rearview before hitting the brakes. My only reliable witness, and he drove right on up the road!" Shock worn off..., he was ticked.

"Where's the idiot?" He stormed over to the driveway.

"So! You're the fool that caused this mess!" The man crossed his arms and faced him.

"What do you mean? All I did was turn in here and park my damn car!" He gave the brim of his straw hat a hard jerk.

"Look here, sonny..., if you blame me..., I'll tell the authorities you had a minor in your truck. How's that suit ya?

Thought I didn't see him, huh? Well I did, so I would think twice if I were you." He walked toward the house, then turned.

"Hell, I think I'll get the cops out here to settle this." Earl shook his fist and glared at him.

"Go ahead! See where it gets you! This was all your fault. You're the idiot who almost got those old people behind you killed, acting like you own the whole damn road! Awh, crap..., ain't no use talking to ya!" Earl dismissed him with a harsh wave, kicked a toe into the gravel, sending pieces flying, then turned and walked back to the road.

Truck righted, road cleaned, he decided he was right.

The man did as he said he would. The judge issued tough, fair options. Earl was reprimanded for following too close and having a minor aboard.

"Son..., you could be sentenced now. This would give you a record and I'd place you on probation.... You've never had a record, seem to be a clean-cut, hard-working fellow, so you have another choice, but I don't want your decision today." The judge paused, cleared his throat, then continued.

"I understand Uncle Sam wants volunteers for the armed services.... Son, you've a choice..., probation and a record, or enlistment into the service of our country. I'll see you back here in two weeks for your response. Court is dismissed."

A. G. Butler stood by him. Earl didn't lose his job, worked hard, and followed company rules the next two weeks. He'd never thought about the service, but now it was constantly on his mind. Everyone had opinions, and Ma's was first.

"If you're smart, young man, you'll take probation and the record. Way things are going in Europe, we're going to be involved at some point. I just know it." Pa's view was direct.

"It's your decision, Son. Do what you feel is right. In 1898, at twenty-two, I was an Army corporal during the

Spanish-American War when America helped Cuba liberate from Spanish rule..., did my part, got through it like any freedom loving man would, and learned discipline, too." Pa hadn't mentioned his past life until now. His words struck deeply into Earl's innermost thoughts. He saw his father in a new light.

In court, he rubbed his jaw as he waited for the judge.

My dad, a corporal.... He shook his head, and grinned.

Well..., if he was a corporal..., Ma's got to be a sergeant..., she's out-ranked him for years! God..., what a messed up pair. No respect for each other, just dominance and fear. Dad puts up with it 'cause he loves us kids and wants us to be a real family. Well..., soon we'll all be gone....

"All rise! This court will come to order."

CHAPTER NINE

BEANS AND HAM AND MAGNIFICENT B-17s

When Earl told his folks of his choice, Ma left the room, face blank. Pa put an arm over his shoulder.

"Well, Son..., make me proud of you." Soon, almost everyone in town knew of the enlistment.

On October 16th, 1941, he was at the recruiting office in downtown Hartford, filling out necessary papers. He was asked which branch he was interested in.

"Army Air Corps, so I can fly, sir." After taking the written exam, a secretary handed him a meal ticket.

"Come back for results after your lunch."

Earl had ordered pie, or a shake, but never a whole meal in a restaurant. He trotted up the street, then entered the eatery.

"Free meal..., can't beat it! Man, hope I passed!" He strode over to the lunch counter, sat on a fancy, bright red, 'spin-till-you're-dizzy' leather-topped stool, and slapped the ticket onto the counter. Music came from back in the kitchen. He tapped the counter, keeping time with 'Oh, Johnny, Oh.'

A nice-looking waitress, hands full of orders, rushed by.

"Sure wish I had a voice like that Wee Bonnie Parker and a nickel for every time she's sung that song!" She set plates down in front of a couple of businessmen, then sped back by. Earl opened his mouth. She smiled.

"Hang onto your seat, hon; be back quicker than you can shake a stick!" She disappeared into the kitchen. He spun about, and saw a young woman stroll by the plate glass window fronting the diner. She wore knee-length paisley print dress, high heels, short fur jacket, and her pretty face was framed by auburn hair caught up in a perky snood. He raised an eyebrow.

"Hmm, not bad! He turned back and forth until the waitress came his way. He knew what to order. She stopped in the dining area at a table surrounded by construction workers and took their orders. His jaw dropped. He tapped the counter.

"Who do they think they are? I was here first!" She finished, then turned. Mouth open, he was ready to order steak, fries, and a huge vanilla shake when, suddenly, another waitress zipped by, grabbed his ticket, and hollered.

"One Army special!" He shut his mouth.

"Sure hope it's steak and fries she's hollering about."

She returned, set a steaming plate in front of him, then hurried off. He eyed it for a couple of long moments, then picked up a piece of cornbread.

"Well...,, I guess beans and ham will do."

"What'dja say, honey?" Same waitress, back with a glass of milk. His ears burned, as she set the glass on the shiny counter. He glanced upward.

Probably old as Ma, and..., chewing that gum the way Greschs' cow chews its cud. Ducking his head, he half-smiled, then looked at her, dead seriousness plastered across his face.

"Uh, I was just saying thanks for the beans and ham." He blinked, then stared, as she smacked her gum and reached to turn the pencil hanging over her left ear. Her smile was bright, but he noticed a couple of front teeth missing.

"You're welcome, hon! Y' have to speak up in here to be heard. Name's Hattie." She snapped a bubble.

"So..., working for Uncle, sugar?" Earl gulped some milk, then filled his spoon.

"Yes, ma'am, Air Corps, I hope. I want to fly..., whoa,

these are hot..., and get a good job after I'm out." He emptied
the spoon, worked the beans over his tongue, then swallowed.

"Man! I'll be here all day!" He slid the plate to a cooler
spot on the counter.

"Wish my son had lived," said Hattie. She sighed. Earl
stole a half-curious look at her. She winked, then smiled a
strange, sad smile.

"Harry's been gone a long time..., accident..., be 'bout
your age now..., had soft-red hair like yours. I mean, you could
be his brother, you look so much like he did. Tell you one
thing..., if he marched in here today and said he was joining,
he'd have my blessing." She patted Earl's shoulder.

"Freedom's important..., damn important. It's all I got
left I can really count on. Take care of yourself, son. Do a
good job and come see me when you get back." Earl nodded.

"Okay..., You've got a deal. Harry was lucky to have a
mom like you." She smiled, touched his cheek, then walked
over to where a nice-looking couple had just sat down.

Earl ate everything on the plate, then ran to the recruiting
office where he fidgeted in a waiting room chair.

The recruiter appeared, took him into his office, then
indicated a chair. Earl sat forward, fingers clenched and
unclenched around well-worn, wooden arms, as he waited for
him to stop shuffling through papers on his desk. He banged the
heel of his boot against the chair leg.

Shoot..., hope he hasn't lost mine. Sure is warm in here.
Wish he'd hurry it up! The officer cleared his throat.

"Congratulations, son. You passed with flying colors.
You're in the Air Corps." Earl breathed a sigh of relief, stood,
and shook the officer's hand.

"Thanks, sir!" The recruiter handed him papers and
something that looked a lot like a movie ticket. Earl smiled.

91

Free lunch, and now a theatre pass.

"Think I'm going to like working for the government.... Whoa..., wait a minute. This says bus fare..., to.... where?"

"Those are your orders, Private Benson. You need to get right over to the bus depot."

Earl's bewildered look was answered with, "My secretary will tell you how to get there."

Everything happened so fast. Barely able to remember the secretary's instructions, Earl ran to the depot.

"Whew! When I started out today, I never thought I'd be going anywhere but here and back home." At the ticket window, he slipped the pass under the bars.

"Do I have time for a phone call?" The clerk stamped it.

"Barely." Earl made a quick call.

"Ma, I don't have time to discuss this. Yes! Army Air Force! The bus is leaving..., I gotta go! Yes, I'll send a card.... Yes, Ma..., I will! Say g'bye to everyone for me."

At Fort Devens, Massachussets, he was issued wrap-leggings and a Smokey the Bear-type campaign hat similar to those issued during World War I. Nothing fit. The hat slid down the sides of his head, forcing his ears to stick out farther than they already did. Indoctrination included more free meals, a medical exam and shots. Stamina and strong back, due to former days of hard work and running, made basic easier.

A letter arrived from home. Howard, nearly twenty-three, had joined the Army.

Upon completion of basic, Earl was promoted to Private First Class, became a drill instructor, and trained recruits in the fine art of marching in step.

He was at Shepard Air Base Sunday, December 7th, 1941, when the Japanese attacked Pearl Harbor. Hearing the broadcast, the nineteen-year-old swore.

"Bastards won't get away with it. We're gonna nail their hides to the walls!"

The next day, President Franklin Roosevelt asked for a Declaration of War on Japan.

Earl Benson - 1942
Shepard Field, Texas

Before Christmas, a letter came. With war declared, Red, almost twenty-two, and Johnny, eighteen, had draft notices.

Christmas away from home was difficult. Earl kept busy, visited with the crew, and overindulged at the Christmas meal in the mess. Many were frustrated at not being home with friends and family. The declaration of war had them confined to base, all leave passes canceled.

That night, Earl's eyes rimmed, as he thought and stared into darkness. He was anxious to get this war over with.

"Bomb the hell out of 'em..., that's what we'll do!"

He worked hard, but was in trouble when the First Sergeant, saw him jump the eternal, unending chow line again.

"Benson..., since you like the consolidated mess so well,

I'm assigning you a real nice job..., a little something to occupy your time here! You're on K.P. for the next two weeks."

Earl spent those seemingly endless days dumping grease pans and scrubbing pots until his arms wanted to fall off. The mess fed fifteen hundred men, each meal, so there was lots of grease and tons of pots to scrub.

Later, he managed to get into the same situation.

Caught again, he was shocked and dismayed when the First Sergeant said, "I'll have your stripe for this incident, Private." Heat crept up the sides of Earl's face.

"This whole thing's unfair, sir! I haven't done anything serious enough to deserve the punishment you're dishing out, but, doggone it, if you want my stripe, you may as well take it."

He took it. Earl learned then how tough the First Sergeant was. Earl thought himself tough. This man was tougher. Earl got smart, real quick, and his duty as a drill instructor went well from then on..., although it still had its trying moments.

He watched a recruit, out of step, head off in the wrong direction during a drill.

"I think it's called payback. It's the Arkansas Kid again, better known as the recruit from hell. This guy's always out of step. I've been on his tail for days and he still hasn't got it right. This is ridiculous!" He confronted the recruit.

"Why the hell can't you manage to keep pace and direction, Private?" he demanded of the tall, lanky recruit, who now stood face-to-face with him. Not batting a lash, Kid looked him straight in the eye.

"Well, Sir..., I followed a mule, plowing all my life.... It had four legs and I was always in step with at least two of 'em."

Another day, Earl saw the uncoordinated recruit leaning against a building, head supported in the palm of his right hand.

Before he could blink, a passing officer received a slouched over, but snappy, left-handed salute. Earl winced.

"Oh, God..., he didn't see it." The officer took two, maybe three, more steps. Reality hit. He stopped in his tracks. Earl's hand came up in front of his mouth.

"Awh..., crap! He saw it. He'll kill him!" He hurried toward the recruit. Then..., it hit him, bringing him to a stop.

"Why am I rooting for him?" He edged closer. Kid still cupped his head in his hand and hadn't moved an inch. The officer, face livid, teeth clenched, glared at the private. Earl shuddered, as the officer shouted.

"Soldier! Why did you salute left handed?" Earl stood to one side, waited for the answer, and watched as Kid's eyes met the officer's stern countenence with the most God-awful..., doleful gaze. He heard Kid drawl.

"Well, sir..., if'n I'da used the right 'un..., I'da plumb fell right on over...."

"Why in hell aren't you standing at attention?" This came from an officer another day. Earl watched from a distance as Kid saluted, noting that at least he'd gotten that part right.

"Sir, I am standin' at attenshun! My clothes are at ease."

Kid's southern twang was heard around base and all over the drill field during the several weeks training. It was an ongoing battle to keep straight-faced order in the platoon.

Off-duty hours were fully appreciated. Payday, once a month, brought about thirty dollars, and Earl often found himself in downtown Wichita Falls after a good meal and a show. With every bit of pride that comes with promotion, he stared at his reflection in windows.

"Yes, siree, that stripe looks real good on my sleeve. He frowned. Been drilling recruits long enough, though. Ain't nothing much to tell when I write home.

95

He volunteered for everything that hit the board. There was need for glider pilots, then paratroupers and gunners. After signing each list, he was called into the adjutant's office.

"Private," said the captain, "your name's on every list that comes through this office. Don't you like it here?"

"Sir, there's a war going on overseas, and I'm still here. I've about decided if I ever have grandchildren, they'll be asking someday about what I did in the war. Hell, Sir, I can't tell them I was just a drill sergeant in Texas!" The captain laughed, and picked up a sheet of paper.

"Well, you're about to get your wish. Says here you're five-feet, five inches tall. That correct?" Earl cocked a brow.

"Yes, sir."

"Weigh a hundred and thirty pounds?"

"One thirty-two, sir," said Earl, fists clenching.

"Hmmn..., they're looking for guys on the small side to train in ball turrets on B-17s, so..., I'm assigning you to gunnery school. Think you can handle that, private?" Earl grinned.

"Yes, sir, you can bet I can, sir! Thank you, sir!"

July 27th, 1942, his twentieth birthday, he was on a train bound for Tyndall Field near Panama City, Florida.

Settling into the routine, he liked training, and learned how to fire all of the guns on a B-17. He learned to field strip a gun, which meant taking it apart and then reassembling it blindfolded. Because of his size, the ball turret position was his assignment. He worked hard, but took time out for fun.

One thing he noticed in Florida was increased heat and humidity. On the Gulf of Mexico, he enjoyed the beach and, late one hot afternoon, found a sandbar, and decided to walk out on it. Signs warning against it were everywhere. He waded in. As the water rose above his knees, he gazed at the view.

"Man, I've never seen a more beautiful sunset." The

reflection of setting sun on water produced a magnificent, kaleidoscopic display. Far out on the bar, the cool water felt good. Small waves lapped against his bare chest. He was wrapped in a hypnotic-like trance, when something in the water a few yards away caught his attention. Eyes snapped into focus.

"Awh..., crap!" Heart pounded into throat as a gray fin headed for him. Arms flailed..., he tried to turn and step away.

"Nnn.. no!" Fear froze him. "Legs....won't....move... Gonna die... gonna be torn apart by a sh...shark! Oh, God! No...!" The ocean boiled up in front of him..., Gray 'monster' rolled, burst from the water, then dove beneath the waves. Arms raised high, then hands clapped to the top of his head, Earl heaved a loud cry of relief.

"Oh...! Oh, my God! Thank You!" He hurried to shore, slipped into his socks and shoes, then looked skyward.

"Whoa...! You do have a sense of humor, don't You? Yeah..., I'll say! Thanks.... for giving me a porpoise to remember for the rest of my life!"

Headed back to camp, he chided himself.

"Benson, you nincompoop! I guess you know..., you will do as signs say, from here on out."

After gunnery training, he was graduated, and promoted to buck sergeant. He rubbed his hands together and grinned.

A step past what Dad was. I want him to be proud. I'll more than keep my word; I'll do better than he'd ever expect.

From Tyndall, he went by train to Casper Air Base in Wyoming to be crewed up and put through more B-17 training.

His first time under a Flying Fortress, his heart raced, and he trembled. He wasn't worried about his shakiness being noticed, though, as the four huge twelve-hundred horsepower engines had been started. The F-model engines, made by Pratt & Whitney or Wright Cyclone, were designed to take the plane

97

with a full load of bombs to thirty-five thousand feet. The shaking fuselage and roar of the engines was impressive and powerful. Peering through the plexiglass of the ball turret, knowing it was his own, Earl tried to memorize every detail.

"Whee, doggies..., I'm a lucky guy! Gonna take down a few enemy aircraft, do twenty-five missions, and come home.... a hero!" They ducked and crouched as the instructor led them into the plane through a rear exit, just after the waistgunners' compartment. They learned that no one was allowed in the tail during take-offs or flights, unless flying into combat. Earl was attentive when told about the six-thousand pounds of bombs, a thousand pounds each, that would be loaded before each mission. They were shown the fifty caliber machine guns. He held one of the waistguns.

"These babies are ready to go.... Wonder how many rounds we'll fire before we've beaten them bastards?"

The pilot of his crew was Lieutenant Charles Thelan, and co-pilot was Lieutenant Raymond Gates. Navigator was Lieutenant Sidney Miller. Bombardier was Lieutenant George Lewis. Buck Sergeant Arnold Hyman was radio operator and a waistgunner. The other waistgunner was Buck Sergeant Arthur Byrd. Staff Sergeant William Hovekamp was engineer and upper turret gunner. Buck Sergeant Clyde Bridges, better known as Stinky, was tailgunner. Earl, a Buck Sergeant, was ball turret and armor gunner, which meant seeing that the rest of the crew kept their guns clean and combat ready. He made sure all guns were maintained and loaded correctly.

At Casper, he flew for the first time. This was exciting for a 'wet behind the ears' kid from a small town, who'd never been 'up there' except for those long ago tree climbing days. He peered down during flights.

What're all those people doing right now? Eating dinner

or getting ready for bed? Wonder how the folks are doing, and all my friends? Are they thinking about me too?

For long flights, box lunches were sent out from the mess. They usually consisted of sandwich, small cake, fruit, and carton of milk, packed into a reclosable cardboard box. Earl savored each morsel, and rarely left a crumb.

"Shoot, far's I can tell, this is better than my mother's cooking ever was. I suppose when you're hungry, though, you'll eat just about anything."

"Where you putting it?" asked Sid Miller, as he passed Earl in the mess hall. Earl patted his stomach.

"Just a growing boy!"

Sid, newly married to a beautiful gal named Barbara, was not stuck on formality of rank. A lot of officers thought they were God's gift, but not him. He invited Earl and the rest of the airmen in the crew to his place for dinner.

Hyman, Hovekamp, Byrd, Bridges, and Benson sat around the elegant table while Barbara served a great-looking chicken dinner. She sat down. They waited for a go ahead sign from Sid. Earl cleared his throat.

Being Jewish, they might say a special prayer. He shifted his weight, scooted closer to the table, then bowed his head.

Barbara smiled and waved a hand at the table.

"Bless this mess. Let's eat, fellas!" They dove in, but..., cutting into the chicken, saw pink. Knowing she was eager to impress them, they didn't let on that it, indeed, was raw, vegetables crunchy, potatos half-baked. They ate everything, then thanked her profusely for a nice evening. Earl wiped his mouth, then laid the napkin beside his plate.

Sid..., Barb..., this is one dinner.... I'll never forget!

The crews flew in training formation to Denver to transport Bob Hope and his entourage to Casper for a USO show. Beautiful, redheaded, Frances Langford was in one plane, with some showgirls. The base commander, with Mister Hope and most of his key people, flew to Casper in the lead plane. Lieutenant Thelan's plane had position behind the lead.

Hope's sidekick must've requested a full tour, because someone in Thelan's crew hollered, "Hey! Get a load! Colona's in the tail!" Jerry was unmistakable, with his heavy black mustache and bugged-out eyes.

At Casper, the airmen were treated to a fantastic show.

Top L to R: Sgt. Andy J. Tenosky, Sgt. Carl E. Frymeyer, S/Sgt. Art Byrd and T/Sgt. William Hovekamp Bottom L to R: Sgt. Earl Benson, Sgt. David Berrensteen, Sgt. Clyde C. Bridges - Casper AFB, Wyoming - 1942

100

L to R: S/Sgt. Clyde C. Bridges, S/Sgt. Earl Benson
Sgt. Al Terwey, Sgt. Arthur Bird
Casper AFB, Wyoming - 1942

Another train trip took Earl to Geiger Field near Spokane, Washington where time was spent at Camp Seven Mile, training in turrets. Upon completion, he returned to Casper.

Thelan's crew flew their plane to Smoky Hill Air Base in Salina, Kansas where Earl was promoted to Staff sergeant. Training finished, the crew was assigned to overseas duty.

Thirteen crews, assigned as a replacement group to fly the first F-models to England, flew to Myrtle Beach, South Carolina, their port of debarkation. Crewmembers waited for orders to fly overseas. Everyone was restricted to base.

Some went to town, and that's where Earl was when new orders arrived, changing the debarkation to Homestead Air Base, below Miami, Florida. The crew left without him.

Earl learned where they were headed, then ran to the field. One of the thirteen B-17s hadn't left, but was starting to taxi to the runway. Earl ran full-out.

"Hey...! Whoa! Wait up!" Banging a fist on the rear compartment, he galloped alongside the lumbering giant.

"Awh..., please! Someone's gotta hear me!" Someone grinned out from the waistgunner's window. Earl waved his hands, flapped his arms, and hollered, as the plane sped up.

"I need a ride to Homestead!" He ran harder.

"Shoot..! Hope he reads lips!" He yelled again. The waistgunner contacted the pilot. The pilot stopped the plane.

"Tell that little s.o.b. we don't mind, but Thelan will..., and tell him to hang on back there, 'cause there ain't a damn chute or nothing on board for him."

Earl made the trip on the number thirteen war plane, hoping he wouldn't need a parachute.

Lieutenant Thelan caught up with him..., didn't take long..., and he was not a happy man. He chewed Earl's butt up one side and down the other.

"Benson, what the hell possessed you to pull a stupid stunt like this? No..., don't answer! I will not tolerate anyone on this crew disobeying orders! You got that?"

"Yes, sir!" The lieutenant glared at him.

"You're on guard duty. You'll guard our plane anytime she's on the ground, unless I relieve you. You got that?"

"Yes, sir!" Earl swallowed hard.

Whew...! Could've lost a stripe on that one!

The rest of the crew gave him a going over.

"God, Benson, the idea of you chasing that bird down the taxi strip just kills me," said Smitty. Sid Miller laughed.

"Yeah, Benson..., from now on..., you're The Rascal Bellygunner!"

"Hey...!" said Bridges. "Naming names, I see everyone's getting 'em painted on their planes."

"Yeah," said Hyman. "We've got to name our bird!"

The F-model was dubbed, 'Bomb Boogie' by Miller, the name, and some musical notes, painted on her nose. Each crewman had a maintainence crew artist paint name or motto outside the plane near his position. Earl chose '1-HUNG LOW,' then watched it formed in white letters outside his turret.

Somehow, Rascal Bellygunner didn't make it. Deserved, or not, he was trying hard to shake the image.

Those magnificent B-17s were entrusted to crews, most in their twenties. That's what they were trained for. Earl, turned twenty in July, knew his duties and how to perform them.

Christmas of 1942 was celebrated at Homestead, his first without snow, or a chill in the air, his second away from family and friends. A huge dinner in the mess filled him, but, his heart was in Unionville.

That night, his thoughts were of his three enlisted brothers, and where they might be by now. The lump in his throat ached.

How are they celebrating?

Up to now, he'd gotten one or two letters a month from his sisters. Christmas cards came, including one from Ma he read, and half-smiled over.

"Huh! I'll be dipped in greased owl hucky! Kenny's married a girl from Hartford, named Helen. That's good news. Guess it eases the homesickness some." He shook his head.

"I've been away from Unionville a whole year, now."

After Christmas, a letter said Ernie had received his draft notice and was in basic training. Earl folded it, then put it in his pocket. "First me, then Howie, then Red and Johnny. Now..., Ernie's in. Uncle Sam's about stocked up on Benson boys."

CHAPTER TEN

THE GREAT DANE ROBBERY

FOUND: One gigantic, friendly Great Dane wandering around the planes on Homestead's airfield. His collar was studded with beadwork and big brass spikes. Earl had to admit this pooch was loveable. It was the first time since Buster had died that he'd allowed himself to bond to another dog. He scratched his new friend behind its ears.

"Since you look like one..., I'm calling you Bull." Bridges and Byrd, wild about him, hid the dog in Bomb Boogie's tail compartment. Hovekamp and Hyman, talked into adopting the pooch, argued about its name. He ended up with five different names, and the gunners took turns sneaking raw hamburger from the mess to feed him. When time to fly overseas, Earl found himself pleading.

"Come on! We can't leave him. It'll break Bull's heart."

"Yeah," said Bridges. "King has to go. He needs us!"

"I'm with Benson and Bridges," said Byrd. "Rex'll be lost without us." Hyman was skeptical.

"Butch should stay here."

"We're outvoted," said Hovekamp. "We'd better get Duke ready. He won't be a problem.... The lieutenant and the rest of the crew rarely go into the back of the plane."

The stowaway was stashed.

Airborne, Lieutenant Thelan trimmed the plane, putting the controls on auto-pilot. The five gunners sat in the cramped radio room, legs crossed, playing poker for cigarettes.

Things were fine until Five Names, who'd been asleep in the waistgunners' compartment, woke, stood, shook himself, then took a leisurely stroll... to the tail. The plane's nose lifted. Thelan, grabbed for the controls. The intercom crackled to life.

"What in hell's going on back there? Whoever's in the tail, get out of there! You're messing up the trim!"

"Yes, sir! We got him, sir! Get him Stinky," said Hyman. Bridges was already tailward.

"Here, King!" He whistled, then returned with it.

"Keep him where we can watch him!" The radio room was cramped. Byrd grabbed the animal by the collar.

"Lie down, Rex!" The gunners settled to the game. Five Names closed his eyes and drifted off to dream.... maybe of rabbit chasing, as he jumped, jerked, and woofed in his sleep.

The game intensified. Earl had a full house, Jacks over sevens, and was fighting to keep a straight face. He sniffed, then coughed, as the most horrific, raunchy odor permeated the entire compartment. Everyone, but the dog, pinched their nose.

"Damn!" Hovekamp moaned, shaking his head.

"Fer crying out loud!" said Byrd though gritted teeth.

"Who's the inconsiderate idiot?" Hyman demanded.

"Not me!" echoed around the group. Everyone shook their heads, and fanned the air. Loud snoring brought realization, all eyes focused on the culprit. Five different voices hollered five different names at the same time.

The noise woke the dog, who wagged his tail as if to say, "Hey! All right! They're talking about me!"

Hyman glared around the group.

"Who's stupid idea was it to bring that mutt with us?" Earl, along with Bridges and Byrd, glared at Hyman.

"Don't go calling Rex a mutt," said Byrd.

"Yeah," said Bridges. "King's our buddy, huh, boy?"

"Darn right," said Earl. "You're a good pup, Bull. Yes you are!" Earl, Art, and Clyde stopped pinching noses, and were now pounding, petting, and stroking the dog's broad back.... Big mistake. Five Names wasn't quiet about it either. The second gaseous assault, deadlier than the first, left everyone gagging. Tears streamed down faces, and everyone fanned.

"Gotta be the hamburger we fed him," said Hovekamp. Bridges snickered, and fanned his own backside.

"Awh, crap! Not you too!" said Byrd. The group glared at him, noses pinched. "For God's sake, don't light a match!"

"Stuff a sock in it, Stinky!" said Hyman. Bridges grinned, then crossed his eyes.

"And just where would you like me to stuff it, Arnolda?" This brought a quick response from Earl.

"Up Bull's yazoo, and your's too, Stinky!" Everyone laughed and, not wanting to be left out, Five Names barked. That settled them down. They got back to the game, but the dog, they were certain, was about to drive them out of the plane.

"I'm telling you," said Hyman, "we're captives! I'm ready to strap our farting friend here into a puppy parachute!"

"Yeah," said Hovekamp, "and I'll show him the door!"

When the plane landed in Trinidad, they managed to sneak Five Names off, and lost him, or, as Earl believed, he lost them, out on the airfield.

The next day, the planes were checked, refueled, and ready for departure. Thelan's crew flew to Belem, a seaport in northeast Brazil, in South America, where they were to refuel and spend another night.

That afternoon, Earl decided to go to town to see the sights, and it didn't take long to convince Byrd and Bridges to go. Hovekamp, not caring to walk through any jungle.... anywhere, volunteered to guard the plane.

Earl strode off, with Byrd and Bridges, down a jungle path and, soon, came across a swampy area at the edge of town.

Naked native children playing in a pond, seemed oblivious to crocodiles sunning themselves on nearby banks. As the men approached, they were surrounded by young, dark-skinned boys with big, dark eyes that glittered with excitement. Chattering turned to broken English as they grabbed the airmen's arms.

"I have pretty.... sister!" said one, grasping Earl's sleeve. "You see! You like sister!" The men were escorted into town which, Earl guessed, was a small village of natives outside the actual city of Belem. Town consisted of nothing but grass huts as far as he could see. He frowned.

"Guys..., we are not in Belem."

Their escorts herded them into the middle of the village, and stopped in front of a grass hut like all the other huts, except for the childish giggling coming from within. With much enthusiasm and determination, the boys shoved their hostages through the small doorway.

Earl's eyes were quick to adjust in the dim lit hut. He stood staring in stunned silence. Byrd coughed..., or was he choking? Bridges whistled. In the middle of the hard-packed dirt floor stood a beautiful, ornate, brass bed. On it were two very young, scantily clad girls.

"Fly boys like good girls?" She giggled, and the other joined in the juvenile twittering. Earl squinted.

"Damn! They're just a couple of kids!"

"You're so right, Rascal." said Byrd. "This isn't Belem."

"Sorta settles it then, doesn't it?" said Bridges. "Let's get the flock outta here."

Outside, they were surrounded. Boys pleaded, danced about, then tried to push them back in.

"You like sisters! Pretty sisters!" The men walked as the boys latched on.

"No!" said Earl, removing a hand from his sleeve. "Absolutely not! No pretty sisters.... No!" The boys wrapped themselves about the men's legs. Byrd and Bridges laughed as they dragged their's along. Earl peeled his set of hustlers off several times as they made their way toward the path at the edge of the village. Several other boys tugged pantlegs and sleeves on the way. Reaching the path, Earl stopped long enough to give each a piece of gum. Appeased, the gang let the airmen go.

It was dusk as the trio made their way back to the field. Heads shaking, they laughed and chided each other for not accepting the generous offer. Byrd clapped Earl on the back.

Did'ja ever think you'd see the likes when they pushed us in there? I about died when I realized what was going on!"

"If the folks back home had seen it..., they would've died!" said Bridges. Earl hooted.

"I can just see Ma's face when she reads my next letter.... Dear Folks..., Today we visited the grass hut of ill repute."

Back at the field, Earl resumed guard duty, assuring Hovekamp he hadn't missed anything by staying put.

On the next leg, Earl slept until Bomb Boogie lost an engine, and they landed in Natal, Brazil.

He was well rested when he began guard duty out on the pitch black field. All was quiet until his ears picked up the sound of footsteps. He tried to ascertain whether this was friend or foe. Metalic clattering and native voices floated through the air. Earl stood alert.

Friends or foe, they're noisy enough. He saw a light and made out more than one figure. The odor of strong, hot coffee made him realize this peculiar procession came from the field cafeteria. It wasn't unusual for workers to bring coffee to help guards stay alert. Next he saw whites of eyes and mouthfuls of pearly-white teeth, as dark-skinned, grinning natives strode up. Intrigued, he noticed they carried gleaming, silver serving trays. Each tray held a complete set of silver creamer, sugar bowl, coffee server and spoons. No one spoke at first. Earl saw that each man wore ornate native clothing and had a short, curved dagger on his hip. With great relish, one poured coffee from the shiny pot into a delicate china cup. Earl added sugar and cream, tasted, and winced.

"Coffee good, sir?" asked the server. Earl dumped it.

"Coffee's strong enough to put a person's hair up on end. This isn't cream, either." The server's expression never changed. He poured more into the cup as Earl tried to return it to the tray, so..., Earl added double sugar, then declined the cream when it was offered again.

"Coffee good, sir?" asked the host again as Earl sipped.

"Ahhh, yes! Thanks! Coffee is much better. Takes some getting used to, though." He grinned at the server. "This sure is an interesting place full of interesting people."

Bowing deeply, his host said, "Very good, sir!"

In Natal, time was spent at a beach, where young boys traded fresh-picked pineapples for cigarettes, candy and gum. Never having tasted pineapple, Earl found it delightful. As he ate it, he noticed a few crewmen up to some fun. They'd taken the fart sacks off their bunks and used them for flotation devices. Earl and his crewmates, thought it a good idea, and brought their bags the next day. The sacks, government issue mattress covers, were made of tight-woven cotton material. Fairly airtight and waterproof, they were like a pillowcase. The men ran along the beach to fill them with air, tied a big knot in the end, then swam out into the ocean to ride waves in.

Naturally, Earl wanted to ride as big a wave as possible,

and swam far out. He was exhilerated and filled with power when a big wave picked him up and carried him toward shore. Pulling hard on the bag, he struggled to get atop, got there, let out a rebel yell, and... the knot came loose. Air forced from the bag, he sank beneath the wave, then surfaced.

"Awh, crap, Benson...! Now you've done it!" He let go of the cover, then swam toward shore. When he'd made some progress, the undertow, like the hand of a vicious demon, pulled him back. Soon he felt the same desperate terror he'd felt as a boy, when he'd almost drowned, but with two distinct differences. One..., he'd learned to swim, though not well. Two..., he remembered that day now as if it was yesterday, and realized how close he was to dying. He yelled to the guys on shore, when not choking, and fought to stay calm.

"Keep swimming..., don't stop!" Water shot up his nose. Fear closed in on determination, and he yelled again. Another wave crashed over his head and he was pulled farther from shore. He waved his hands, and screamed.

"Freakin' idiots! Sitting there, going on with your fun..., Now is not the time to assume I'm kidding with you, guys!" Another wave crashed over him. He flailed his arms.

"Oh, God! I don't want to die!" Someone... waved, and that did it. Renewed strength pulled him through the water.

"No good sons-a-bitches! If I manage to get there, I'll break every last one of your damned necks!" Every muscle, strained to the limit, forced him closer to shore.

"Almost there.... gotta make it...." He reached a toe down and felt sand. Pulled back again, he felt it slide between his toes.

"No...! Oh, God! Help me!" Every move instinctive, he fought the relentless undertow. Several times, sand slipped from beneath his feet. Then..., he got a toehold, and another, and one

111

more he wasn't about to lose.

"You.... ain't.... beating me! I didn't come this far just to drown.... in some damn ocean!" He floundered, exhausted, rubber-legged, toward the beach, arms and legs like lead weights, heart pounding in his chest, breath coming in shuddering gasps.

"Idiots! Didn'tcha see me drowning out there?" He let the whole crowd see his anger, then collapsed onto the sand. Shaking, knees bent, forehead down on kneecaps, he sat, arms wrapped about ears, red face hidden, hot tears rimming his eyes. He struggled to catch his breath as Byrd and Bridges stood near.

Byrd knelt.

"God, Rascal, I'm sorry! We thought you were joking around..., figured you were up to your pranks again."

"Yeah," said Bridges. "How were we to know you were really in trouble?" He touched Earl's shoulder.

"Sorry, Rascal. You okay, now?" Covering both eyes with the palms of his hands, Earl raised his head, inhaled, then held the breath as if holding onto life itself. He exhaled, pulling hands and fingers down his face, then looked at his friends.

"That was too damn close...! Water.... is not my friend..., I mean..., how can you battle something that big?" He waved a hand, indicating the ocean before them. "This guy's staying close to shore from now on."

At the field, the rest of the crew heard about it.

"So, Rascal," said Hyman, "the ole fart sack let you down, huh?" Everyone laughed, and soon had a song made up.

"He's a rascal bellygunner, his fart sack let him down. If he don't make it in to shore, he's surely gonna drown!" Adding disgusting armpit sound effects, they danced around.

When Thelan heard, he laid an arm over Earl's shoulder.

"I should put you on restriction to keep you out of

trouble, Benson.... I swear..., someone up there is watching out for your sorry ass.... His voice was harsh and, as he continued, Earl felt ice-cold chills shoot through him.

"I did not bring you this far.... just to lose you in some damn ocean!"

Bomb Boogie's lost engine kept the crew in Natal for several days. When two or more planes were disabled, pilots tossed coins to see who'd give up a working replacement part from his plane to fix the winner's ailing craft. One pilot lost coin tosses until his B-17 was minus all four engines. Thelan won his toss, and they were on their way again.

This leg of the trip was to Dakar, the capital of Senagal, West Africa. During the flight, they were fortunate they had a good navigator in Miller. Anxious to get to England, Thelan had been told by Sid they could make up lost time, flying a direct route from Natal to Dakar. This meant not stopping to refuel in the Ascension Islands. By the time they neared their destination, Bomb Boogie was running on fumes, and Thelan was on the intercom.

"This bird had better make it, Miller..., or I'm going to personally feed you to the sharks."

"She'll make it, sir. No sweat!"

Runway spotted, Lieutenants Thelan and Gates shut down two engines to conserve fuel, and landed on a runway of steel mats laid out on dirt. As Bomb Boogie taxied in, the third engine quit. As she slowed to a stop, the last engine sputtered and died.

Thelan looked pale, paler than the rest of the crew, as they walked away from the plane. Earl overheard muttering.

"Damn it, Miller! Don't ever pull a stunt like this again!"

Earl wiped an arm over his brow. "Man...! Dakar's hot! I've never been this warm! Big lizards skittered everywhere.

The crew slept on the plane, as provisions were zero. They laughed when Thelan, passed blankets around.

"Going to be a cold night, fellas." Earl shook his head.

"Awh, come on! Heat's been unbearable all day. It can't get that cool!"

It was frigid, and they could've used a couple more blankets. Teeth chattering, they put on their sheepskin-lined winter flying suits, wrapped up in the now fully appreciated blankets..., and were still cold.

The next day, Earl met a crewman from another plane who'd bought a monkey from a native. Cute little guy..., the monkey that is. Earl was fascinated.

What's his name?

"Monkey.... Got any candy or gum? He really likes gum." Earl took out a piece, but before he could unwrap it, the little snitch grabbed it. Earl tried to retrieve it, to remove the wrapper, and that did it.

Monkey clomped down hard on Earl's finger. Earl yanked his hand back.

"Damn..., bugger bit me!" Still neatly wrapped, the gum disappeared into the animal's mouth. Earl swore.

"Sucker nailed me!" Mouth open, he held the injured finger with his other hand, then moved closer again. Monkey shrieked and glared. Earl put his hands up.

"Whoa! I'm not pursuing this relationship any further..., and I'm sure not offering anything to any monkey again!"

The next leg was to take them from Dakar to Casa Blanca, but they were re-routed to Marrakech, a major trade center in French Morocco because German Field Marshall, Erwin Rommel was near Casa Blanca.

To Earl, Marrakech was a place right out of The Arabian Nights, with narrow twisting streets full of markets. Byrd and

Bridges wandered the marketplace with him.

Earl bought a bottle of liquor, and the gunners shared it as they looked at the array of wares. Women passed, wearing veils covering olive-skinned faces.

Native men wore turbans, and had long, curved knives strapped to their hips. Earl approached one, and asked to see his. He was reluctant, but Earl convinced him. The weapon, drawn from a handsome leather scabbard set with beautiful jewels that sparkled in the sunlight, was held in front of them, sharp blade gleaming.

"Man!" said Earl, almost touching it, "I'd like to own this sweet thing!" The man moved away.

"No sell." Concern remained on his face, even after the trio had finished admiring the handsome piece. Earl thanked him, then the amazed airmen watched the man pull the edge of the blade across his thumb, somber expression unchanged. Tradition demanded, when a weapon was drawn, the owner must draw blood. Ruby-red, glistening, it stood still a moment, as they stared, transfixed, then a trickle ran to the tip of his thumb and fell to the dust. He wiped the blade, then slid the knife back into its scabbard. It was his to be proud of and not for sale to flying Americans.

Earl found the marketplace intriguing, shopkeepers friendly and insistant. He was talked into buying a pair of handmade slippers. Inlaid with silver, intricately embroidered, toes pointed, they stunk to high heaven because the leather hadn't been properly cured.

The flyers, especially Bridges, were feeling the effects of the alcohol, when they stumbled across a brothel. Clyde, eighteen and a true virgin, was fixed up with a girl, while Art and Earl stood outside and finished the bottle.

Later, they had a devil of a time as Clyde repeated over

and over, "Hot damn! Gotta go do that again!" He swaggered and grinned all the way back to the plane.

"Know what, fellas...? I ain't never.... gonna forget Marrakechhhhh...!" Before they could get him out of town, Earl and Art were confronted with a comical sight.... Moroccans next to baskets of fruit, wearing what looked like blue barracks bags for britches. They approached and found that the pants were, indeed, barracks bags, and the men would barter for more.

They took Clyde to the field and left him in the plane to sleep it off. He mumbled as they made him comfortable.

"Back... do 'er... 'gain...." Rounding up several bags, they rushed to town, and worked out the transaction.

Delighted natives cut holes in the bottom of each bag, climbed in, cinched the drawstrings tight, then, arms loaded, followed Earl and Art back to the field.

Thelan's crew waited a couple of days for clear weather before flying to England. The crew flew in positions, guns loaded, because the Germans were flying out of Africa. German fighters were a threat. U-boats were spotting American planes, but Thelan's crew had no run-ins.

They reached the airfield near Southhampton, England fifteen days after leaving the States. A Royal Airforce crew, that included several women, met them, and helped get the planes parked by chalking tires and such. When the ladies popped open the door to Bomb Boogie's tail section, oranges, tangerines and bananas tumbled out. They shrieked, laughed, danced about, and Thelan's crew was about hugged to death. With severe rationing, it was near impossible to get fresh fruit. Earl had never seen a happier group and was kissed twice.

It was a wonder Bomb Boogie had made it. Her tail was packed. The heavy odor of tangy, ripe citrus and bananas permeated the interior. The gunners had eaten more than they

116

should, and were lucky to have maintained good constitutions during the flight. The airmen held on to what was left and took it with them when they flew to Thurleigh Royal Air Force Base near Bedford, England, the 306th Bombardment Group's base.

No longer Thelan's, Bomb Boogie was reassigned to the 91st Bomb Group. At Thurleigh, the crew took additional training and was indoctrinated into the system, learning what was to be, who they'd be with, and where they were going. Gunners took refreshers on combat tactics, which taught them where to look for enemy planes and what to expect during battle. They learned that, for the first five missions, the crew would be split, most being placed with more experienced crews.

Between missions and courses, there was recreation. Activities included baseball, basketball, darts, billiards, and dances at the NCO club. Loads of English girls were bussed to the base to enjoy dances with the men.

Earl made it to town once in awhile. In Bedford, in a little restaurant, he ordered Welsh Rarebit. Meal served, he poked at it..., pushed toast and melted cheese around the plate.

"Where is it?" He lifted the bread and peered beneath it.

"No rabbit under here, either. Huh...! I'll be dipped!" A waiter came over. Earl looked into his pale, pinched face.

"Could I have a napkin?" He listened, then..., red faced, as the server whispered in his ear.

"Sir..., you are designating an item.... which is used quite uniquely and.... very discretely, by British women..., for feminine protection."

Thus began Earl's education of England's sometimes strange and rather distinct culture and cuisine.

While at Thurleigh, some of the crew went to London. As bombs fell, Earl and his buddies sat in a pub, in the Picadilly Circus area, during the blackout, drinking gin and tonics. It was dark and quiet between shellings, then..., the building shook, and they were about knocked off of the bar stools.

Earl repositioned himself, then downed his drink.

"Man...! This stuff packs a punch!"

His first bombing mission was March 22, 1943. Thelan's crew flew tail-end-Charlie. With limited fuel capacities, English Spitfires escorted bombers across the English Channel, then returned to base. The formation flew unescorted to the target, which was Wilhelmshaven, a seaport in Lower Saxony, northwest Germany, on the North Sea, an important naval base. The target was sub pens, underwater construction/maintainence garages for German submarines made of concrete about four feet thick on all sides. The group of about thirty B-17s pounded the hell out of the pens with about eighteen thousand pounds of bombs. German fighters attacked, like swarms of angry hornets, some barrel rolling though the formation. Wings lit up as they fired guns with the intent of crippling as many 17s as possible. If they forced one to leave formation, they ganged up on it until it was shot down. Earl fired bursts when possible.

"Damn! Can't get a clean shot!" To his left, oxygen tank hit, a B-24 exploded into a ball of fire. In a split second, the pilot was a black silhouette, outlined against the cockpit window, then, in a blinding flash, the plane blew apart and fell from the sky. Earl shook off the horrific vision.

"God...! Poor bastards never knew what hit 'em." His eyes scanned from his position in the turret.

"Damn...! Flak's so thick, you could walk on it!" He spotted a Messerschmitt a thousand yards out behind him, and spun the turret as it flew across the sky, side to side, right to left, a difficult shot. He lined up the nose of the enemy plane in the crosshairs of his sight.

"Son-of-a-bitch thinks he's home free." He fired a couple

of short bursts.

"You can do this, Benson." Smoke spewed from the Messerschmitt's engine.

"Nailed him!" The plane dove, then spiraled downward. He didn't see if the pilot got out, as two more enemy planes flew in, guns firing, and were knocked from the sky before he had a chance at them.

After landing at Thurleigh, each remaining crew was debriefed separately about the mission. An officer debriefed Earl's crew, then scratched his head over the paper he held.

"Sergeant Benson..., are you the ball gunner on this crew?" Earl stood, felt everyone's eyes on him, and reddened.

"Yes, sir." He stared straight ahead at the officer.

"Haven't you something to tell me?"

"Well..., no, sir, not that I know of." The officer frowned, then cleared his throat.

"Well, Mister..., two or three crews saw you take out a German fighter..., with one hell of a good shot, I might add..., so it's confirmed. Congratulations. You'll receive your Air Medal soon. Dismissed!"

Earl hadn't wanted to seem a glory-seeker out for medals on his first mission, but, now..., he was bursting with pride.

"Man, oh, man. Finally..., something exciting to write home about. Wait'll my father hears about this!"

Earl's second bomb run was March 28, 1943. The target, Rouen, a port city in northwest France, on the Seine River. Spitfires escorted the B-17s across the channel, then the flying fortresses were on their own. The marshaling yards were bombed successfully and, after intense fighting and manuvering, most of the planes returned safely.

His third mission, bombing Rotterdam, took place March 31st. Was his crew to always wind up flying tail-end-Charlie, the most dangerous position in the formation? It made their plane a significantly better target for enemy fire. Fighting was fierce and, again, his crew made it back.

April 4th, they flew over Paris, France and hit the marshaling yards. During the mission, Earl, tried talking the bombardier into taking out the Eiffel Tower.

"We'd be famous, for sure!" Rascal was in a bad mood.

"If we can't be down there enjoying some sightseeing, good food, and girls..., well, hells bells, Paris might as well not be there, far as I'm concerned."

The formation was attacked, another intense battle with enemy fighters, and the group lost a couple planes. Earl was anxious for the first five missions to be over.

"Then our crew can get back together, complete twenty more, and go home. We'll be heros!" He felt good when he found that Hyman, Hovekamp, Byrd, Miller, Lewis, and big Raymond Gates, a farm boy from around Downs, Kansas, almost all of them original crew, would be with him on the fifth mission. They'd be flying with Lieutenant Kelly Ross and two others, Sergeant Douglas Bowles, a radio operator, and Sergeant Clyde Smith, a waistgunner.   Art Byrd drew tailgunner position, as Clyde Bridges was sick.

"Yes, sir, we've got this fifth mission..., then our crew will go out there and show all the others how to win this war!" In the back of his mind loomed the fact that had been stated many times by other crewmen.... the average number of missions for any B-17 combat crew..., was five..., before they'd be shot down and captured or, worse yet, killed. The 367th Bomb Squadron was aptly named, The Clay Pigeon Outfit.

CHAPTER
ELEVEN

THE FIFTH MISSION

Twenty bombers flew out of Thurleigh toward their intended target, the Erla Works, a Ford factory in Antwerp, Belgium. Ross' crew of ten, counting himself, was ready. Earl scanned the skys from his turret, and talked to himself.

"Squadron looks good and strong this morning. Neat, the way the light reflects across the sky..., real pretty." Nearing the target area, he watched for the enemy.

"Had good action my last four missions.... What will they hit us with today? Well, it doesn't matter, 'cause I'm ready....

"Bogies!!" Fighters were on them before they could reach the target and drop the load of bombs. The elite Luftwaffe hit hard. Earl counted seven fighters queuing up in front of them. Wings lit up as they came in. Folkerwolfes barrel rolled through the formation. Ross shouted into his headset.

"Bogies, twelve-o'clock low! Get 'em, bellygunner!" Earl tracked, spun the turret, fired several bursts, and knocked two fighters from the sky. More came in from a direction that made him realize the guys up front were having trouble getting shots at them. Ross was counting on Hovekamp in the upper, and Earl in the lower turret, to make the shots. Earl lined one up.

"Come 'n get it, ya Nazi bastard!" Bullets bounced off the rounded metal of the turret, shaking it with sharp vibrations. Relief swept through him when the fighter went down. The enemy knew the angle to use. Fighter after fighter came in, eleven and twelve o'clock level, disabling two engines. It was almost impossible to fire back because of interrupters on the guns, which kept crews from shooting props off of their own planes. Ross' B-17 lagged behind the formation.

"Bogies, twelve o'clock high! Upper turret, why aren't you firing? Fire! We get the bastards off our backs, we'll go home tonight!" Hovekamp responded.

"Can't, Sir! Vibration'll break the windshield!"

"To hell with the windshield! I ordered you to fire!" Hovekamp laid the big guns down tight against the cockpit roof. The panels vibrated over Ross' and Gate's heads as he knocked two fighters from the sky. Ross bulled the nose of the plane up and down to give upper and lower gunners better advantage. He was out of formation, and the group behind them was too far back to give any cover.

Communication between Benson, Ross, and Gates was uninterrupted until a twenty millimeter cannon shell exploded to Ross' left. It hit in the leading edge of the wing, leaving him no rudder, aileron, throttle, or intercom. Gates took over at his set of controls. Ross saw the formation make a left turn.

"Only one way this bird's gonna catch up." He leaned toward Gates. "Left turn! Let's try to cut 'em off at the pass!"

It became apparent..., there was no way of making this happen. Fear clutched at the lieutenant's stomach. He realized the Luftwaffe was about to have a field day.

"We're losin' it, Ray!"

"Not if I can help it," muttered Gates, bulling the nose up. Miller yelled into the intercom.

"Take 'em down, Benson!" Earl downed the fighter.

"Yeah! Way to go, rascal! Keep after the lousy bastards!" A twenty millimeter whizzed by Sid's ear, and exploded against the oxygen tank. Shouting erupted as Ross,

Hovekamp, and Bowles were hit with schrapnel. Miller heard loud hissing as oxygen leaked from the big tank. It should've exploded, he knew that. He'd seen planes explode into a million pieces. Ross, stunned, a piece of skull ripped away, fell onto the control panel. The plane shuddered..., rolled, then dove.... straight down.

White-faced, pinned in his seat, Earl couldn't lift a finger.

"We're... not... gettin' outta... this!" Someone had told him that before a person died, their whole life flashed before their eyes. Rascal knew, now, it was true. As he plummeted toward death, every bad thing he'd ever said or done confronted him. In horrifying, endless seconds, Mister Moses cried pitifully, his grotesque, wizened face contorted before Earl's..., there in a millisecond..., gone in a flash. Scenes he couldn't begin to describe, one after another, whipped through his mind, shaking him to the bottom of his soul.

As the plane dove, Miller, fighting hysteria, was filled with a calming presence, sensed distinctive perfume, spoke to it.

"Oh..., Barbara! I'm dying....! I'll never hold you again!" Her comforting voice filled his head.

"I'm with you, darling.... Hold on. It'll be okay."

Gates had Ross. Forcing him off the controls, he planted both feet against the panel..., and hauled back on the column. Muscles strained to the limit, the co-pilot struggled and prayed.

Seven..., eight..., nine thousand terrifying..., shuddering feet..., straight down, then..., in the next thousand feet, she leveled out. Gates wiped his brow as Ross regained his senses.

Earl, spotted a yellow-nosed Folkerwolfe-190, spun the turret, then fired for what seemed an eternity, into the nose and cockpit of the fighter as it closed in.

"Still coming!" The 190 was three hundred yards out.

"Jesus! He's headed for our cockpit!" Earl fired.

123

"Go down!" A twenty millimeter penetrated the Plexiglass of his turret, spun around the inner glass, then dropped between his knees to the floor.... without exploding. He didn't see, as much as he heard and sensed, its imminent proximity. Focused on the advancing fighter, holding it in the crosshairs of his automatic sight, he kept firing. The intercom crackled, as Gates screamed.

"Take him down!"

Two hundred yards.... The German pilot, poised in his cockpit, headed for a direct hit into the nose of their B-17.

"Gonna sacrifice...! Go down...!" screamed Earl.

A hundred yards.... Earl braced, and fired.

"Gonna hit us! Oh, God...!" The sky exploded into a brilliant flash, a blinding ball of fire, as the 190 disentegrated. Earl kept firing, terror ripping his soul to shreds as he waited for his turret to be wiped from beneath the belly of the plane. A shell exploded, louder than thunder, next to his turret, shattering Plexiglass, leaving his ears ringing. Shards and schrapnel peppered hands, legs, face and chest. Searing heat from engine fires, spatterings of boiling hot oil, hit him. One gun, bent to hell, wouldn't fire. He picked out another Folkerwolfe and, with the remaining gun, fired until it went down.

Dense smoke, oil, and heat from the fires was unbearable. Forced to turn, he fired in any direction except forward. When the turret spun too far around, he was burned again.

Hovekamp took out two fighters as they came into his line of fire. Up front, Miller fired, then, yelled.

"Can't get a shot at the bastards! We can't take these head-on assaults much longer!"

In his cockpit, Ross knew they couldn't keep the ship airborn. The intense battle had taken thirty, maybe forty minutes. Lowering the wheels, he nodded at Gates....

"Tell the crew to bail."

At nine thousand feet, in what seemed an unbelievably calm demeaner, Lieutenant Gate's voice crackled in Earl's ear.

"Well boys..., this is it. We're going down. You'd better get out." Earl twisted the grips of his controls forward to move the turret hatch inside the plane. It was barely in position when the power went out. He unfastened his lap belt, turned the latch, opened it toward the rear and, rubbery-legged, pushed upward. As his head popped up behind it, a twenty ripped through Hyman's midsection, and exploded against the outer side of the hatch. Covered with Hyman's blood, and his own, Earl tore out of the turret, then peered at the waistgunner.

"Dead.... Awh, shit! He's dead...! No one could've survived that...." Black smoke filled the compartment. With the intercom out, he wasn't sure the others had heard the order.

"Bail out! Everybody out!" Grabbing his chute, he snapped the chest pack onto the D-rings of his harness, then fought his way toward the bailout door. Shells flew by, from every direction. Light filtered into the compartment through countless holes.

Wide-eyed, Miller looked up at Ross. The lieutenant gave him a thumbs down, the order to bail. Miller stepped away from his gun. As he went for the escape hatch, the area he'd been in was riddled. Gun, frame, Plexiglass, all of it, wiped out, in a barrage of gunfire. All four engines were disabled. The hatch wouldn't open. Sid kicked it loose and exited the plane. The plane was about to go out of control.

At the rear exit, Earl found Clyde Smith..., frozen in front of it. Explosions rang through the plane, as shells exploded around them. Earl yelled, and shook the unresponsive gunner.

"Smitty, we gotta get outta here!" Smith stared straight ahead. Earl shoved him aside, then reached for the bright red release handle.

"Gone...! Shot the hell out...! Smit couldn't get it open!
Must be in shock.... Get out....! Oh, God, we gotta get out!"
Earl turned toward the tail, smoke burning eyes and throat.

"Byrd! Art's not forward! Must be hurt bad..., or dead!
Gotta get the hatch open..., get out...! Smitty! Bail!" Stepping
back, he pounded the gunner's chest with a hard fist, then
slapped him hard across the face.

"We're gettin' outta here! Move your ass!" He shoved
Smith further to the side, then, with everything left in him...,
hurled himself feet first at the hatch.

He flew out, yelling, door and all. Violent wind ripped
his hand across his chest, the horizontal stabilizer missed his
head by less than an inch, the chute opened with a vicious jerk.

Is my chute caught? New chutes, issued a day before,
were twenty-four feet, instead of twenty-eight. Ribs snapped...,
he passed out.

Coming to, he looked up to see his chute, full of holes,
damaged by enemy fire while in the waistgunners' compartment.
Shroud lines flew loose; several dangled in the air. Staring at
the canopy, he drew in a sharp, painful breath.

"Man..., it looks like swiss cheese!" Frigid wind whipped
at him. Relieved to be out of the flying coffin, he didn't think
about the fact that he was descending faster than anyone else.
Though he hadn't meant to be, he was one of the first out of the
dying bird. He hollered and waved at a couple of crewmates,
then cheered when he saw others exit the floundering fortress,
chutes opening safely.

Fighters dove, just above their chutes, trying to collapse
them by swooping overhead and sucking air from the canopies.

"Stinking cowards!" yelled Earl, as one swooped from
above. His descent was too fast for the attempt to be successful.

He shook his fist, remembered his shoulder holster, felt for and found the forty-five..., thought about firing at the fighter....

No time. Earth was about to be encountered.

"Whoa.... baby! Hope I hit something soft!" Training kicked in. Drifting over water, he prepared to unfasten snaps holding his harness snug about each thigh, as he'd been trained to do if landing in water. Wind pulled him back over land.

Wait, Benson.... Back over water again, he bent, tongue halfway out of his mouth, and reached for the snaps....

Too late. Water rushed up at him. He hit, and felt as if he'd struck a brick wall. He'd not managed to unsnap snaps or pull tongue back into mouth. There was no chance to be dazed as the shocking, cold water of the Schelde River swallowed him.

He surfaced, under the chute, gasping. Bone-chilling cold added to pain, shot through broken ribs, as he fought to keep his head above water.... He reached down, unsnapped the snaps, untangled himself, and fought to stay above water.

Saltwater burned into wounds; he tasted blood..., felt his tongue swelling, having bitten it nearly in half.

"I'm in the bay. Man..., good I didn't hit ground..., would'a killed me!" In the effort to stay afloat..., he swallowed what he thought was half the bay of Antwerp.

"God, it's icy! Oh..., my tongue!" He deployed his Mae West. Once it was aired, he swam toward a dike, a hundred yards, or so, until he touched bottom. He stood..., drawing in short breaths, as broken ribs rubbed against one another. Glancing shoreward, he spotted a handful of German soldiers standing on the dike. One wagged a finger in a come hither gesture. The rest stood, guns pointed.

"Up your pututies...!" Earl worked his arms out of the Mae West, tossed it aside, then removed his shoulder holster.

One of the soldiers shouted.

"Nein...!" Earl's jaw hardened.

"Bullcrap! This is one they're not getting. He dropped the forty-five into the water..., took two steps toward them..., then swallowed the other half of the bay. In over his head, he surfaced, choked, cleared his throat, then swam for his life.

He made it to the dike, coughing, gasping for air, crawled up the grassy bank, struggled to his feet, reached into his shirt pocket for a cigarette, found them dripping wet, and hurled them up the embankment.

"Damn!" A soldier grabbed them, and put them into his own pocket. A ferocious-looking police dog's bark was sharp and continuous, as it strained against its leash. Guns drawn, two soldiers stepped to each side of Earl. A third, gun in one hand, confiscated his survival pack, handing it to another soldier.

"Ceegahrette?" Smile cold, he extended a pack. Earl nodded, then tried to keep from shaking as the soldier offered a light. Inhaling, to calm nerves and ease pain, he choked on the strong, cigar-like tobacco. Doubled over, ribcage cradled, he coughed and moaned. Two officers strode up. One spoke.

"English?" Earl winced, shook his head no.

"Ahh...! Americano!" Heels clicked smartly together. Stiff fingers pointed skyward.

"For you, the vor ees ofar! Heil, Hitler!"

Earl was escorted to where crew and squadron members were being loaded onto several trucks.

Sid Miller's chute broke his ribs; he felt as if he'd been shot. Landing in mud up to his knees, his back caved in and he was knocked out for a short time. In excruciating pain when he came to, he dug into his survival pack for energy pills.

"Got to stay awake and alert." Soon, though, he was hallucinating and dizzy. At one point, sure he could fly over the dike, he flapped his arms, jumped into a ditch, and found himself up to his neck in muddy water. He had consumed water purification tablets, and by the time civilians had him and his forty-five in custody, he was yelling.

"Hey, I'm a Jew! Hey, you..., yeah, you, man! You gonna shoot me?" A young man demanded his wedding band. Miller sneered, then refused. The young German pointed his gun at Sid's head, and repeated the demand. Miller laughed.

"Minutes ago, I was shot at with twenty millimeters, so your stupid little toy gun doesn't impress me at all!" An officer stepped in and put an end to the dispute.

With Earl as their only prisoner, his captors took over a Belgian couple's farmhouse. Directed about at gunpoint, the man was taken to another room while his wife was ordered into the kitchen to cook. Earl was prodded into the kitchen, then directed toward a corner near the table.

Ross' plane was downed mid-morning, the day begun at dawn, the mission early. Exhausted, Earl cradled his ribs and eased onto the floor. He hadn't eaten since then, and the odor of food was a reminder. He glanced up to where the woman, probably in her late twenties, stood, hands shaking, filling plates for the Germans. Earl realized he wasn't to be fed. Pointing and gesturing, he asked for his pack. A soldier handed it over. Earl took the concentrated chocolate D-bar, unwrapped it, broke it, then ate a piece. The woman, finished at the stove, knelt and took his hand into hers. For a long moment, she gazed at him..., then blue eyes flooded with tears.

"You are so young!" Earl offered a piece of chocolate. Touching it to her lips, she tasted its sweetness with the tip of her tongue..., and held tight to his hand.

The officer, mouth full, spotted her. Dishes clattered as he pounded the table. Throat cleared, he yelled. She jumped up. He yelled again, waved an arm at her, and she fled from the room. Snatching the survival pack from Earl's lap, he hurled it across the room, then glared at him. Earl eyed him, then leaned into the corner, closed his eyes, and wished the pain would stop.

Just one breath without hurting, please... his mind begged.

He dozed, only to awaken every few minutes, unable to remember where he was, until pain reminded him. He sat, knees drawn to chest, hugging them, hoping for relief. Curled into the corner, he waited..., waited for the door to be broken in..., waited for a roomful of American soldiers to gather him up and take him back to England..., waited for them to tell him he was going home..., waited for the pain to stop. He shivered. Dressed in khaki shirt and pants under flying coveralls, he'd not been given opportunity to dry them. Heat from the stove gave little comfort, as he wasn't near it.

The Germans tried interrogation, but none spoke English. One obnoxious character demanded information using gestures and sound effects.

Over and over, he pretended he was cranking a prop, then said something that sounded to Earl like, "Uhhmmm, blugh, blugh, blugh." He pointed emphatically at his watch.

"Wieviel uhr?" Earl understood.

Bastard wants me to tell him what time we took off, how long we flew, and when we dropped our bombs, so he can report it and be a hero. After each barrage of questions, he looked wide-eyed at the soldier, then shrugged.

"I don't understand." The German glared at him.

"Nicht verstehen?" Earl glared back at him.

 Nope. I don't understand, dummy.

"Du ein gross fliegenganster. Schweinhund!" Earl shrugged again.

So, I'm a flying gangster and a pigdog. What else is on your mind, idiot? He leaned back and closed his eyes. The

German humped out of the room.

As the day wore on, Earl grew colder. His teeth chattered and his body shook in uncontrollable spasms. He struggled, trying to gain comfort.

God, make them take me to a hospital or bring me a doctor! He stretched a leg out, then pulled it back.

Not gonna happen.... Okay, relax..., can't think about pain.... He huddled, miserable, in the corner, shaking subsiding a little as he stared at a sunspot on the floor. Imagine yourself in it, Benson, warm, cozy..., no pain... and... Oh, God, it's no use!

The vision of his brother's fiddle, smashed into so many pieces, occured to him, and it was as if it had taken place yesterday. Earl whispered to himself.

"Oh, Kenny...!" he drew in a sharp, painful breath... "Oh, God, brother, if only you were here.... and could put me back together..., good as new...." he sucked in an agonized breath, eyes rimming with tears.... "and just take me.... home...!"

He heard voices outside.

"Truck engines...."

TWELVE

REVELATIONS

A high ranking officer clicked through the house, shouting orders. A guard kicked and shoved Earl to his feet. Another prodded him out the door. Earl was relieved when, upon reaching a truck, the guard nodded at the driver, opened the passenger door, and helped Earl up into the seat. The unusual display of care went farther when he climbed in, rested the barrel of his gun across Earl's lap, then handed him a cigarette. Earl noted the trucks were Ford stake body-types. Sockets fitted with stakes supported railings which now surrounded American prisoners as they rode in the backs of the trucks.

Separated from his crew, Earl hoped they were okay. The guard drove at a good clip to keep up with the truck ahead. Bounced along, Earl was thankful to be in the cab. Still, he grimaced in agony with each jar, and tried, in vain, to prepare for the onslaught of bumps and ruts.

The trucks stopped at an airfield near Antwerp. The guard helped him out, then directed him and others to a building.

Inside, Earl was led by one guard and pushed by another. Brows knotted, glancing about the crowded room, he spotted Hovekamp and other crewmembers.

Unbelievable.... Looks like the Germans put together a reunion of the whole damn 306th! A few more steps, and his heart leapt into his throat.

Thelan! Oh, God! The lieutenant's plane went down!"

Earl's heated boots had been jerked off when his chute

had opened. The soldiers had given him a pair of wooden shoes that must've come straight from Holland. Now he clip-clopped as he entered a room where a couple of female secretaries sat typing at desks. Handed dry pants and shirt, he was told to put them on. He eyed the women.

Well..., they've likely seen it all before, anyway. Told to take fur-lined winter flying boots from a pile, he took a pair and set them by a chair. The clothing was made of rough pressed fibers. He pulled on the pants.

Least they're dry. About to slip on the boots, he spotted something in the right one. A quick glimpse allowed it was a compass. He slid his size seven foot in, pushed the compass to one side, and hoped it wouldn't become too uncomfortable.

I'll put you in a better place soon, my friend. He sat down on the chair, holding his damp clothes.

Soon, an interrogator paced back and forth in front of him, wearing horn-rimmed, coke-bottle-thick glasses, speaking perfect Oxford English.

"Good evening, Sergeant Benson. It is most certainly an unfortunate atrocity that you and your comrades have become our prisoners today, but that is how it is..., and must be." Earl eyed the pompous strider.

"Sergeant Earl Benson, no middle initial, born Unionville, Connecticut, the twenty-seventh of July, 1922, ball turret gunner on plane number 42-29660. Took gunnery training at Harlingen, Texas." Earl almost corrected him, but caught himself.

Bastard's got all but Tyndall Field right. How in hell did they find out so much? That came straight from my records. Had to! I don't know how, but it ticks me off. This half-blind, beak-nosed, arrogant asshole's having himself a real good time with this. The German confronted him.

"Isn't this so, Sergeant Benson?" Earl wasn't carrying

anything German intelligence could gain from.

He didn't wear a watch, and gave his wallet to the crew chief at Thurleigh, saying, "Keep the money if I don't get back."

Shoot...! Bet he's out spending my eighteen pounds this very moment! Earl eyed the interrogator, but didn't respond.

"What do you say, Sergeant Benson?" The man was in his face. Earl scowled up at him.

"Staff Sergeant Earl Benson." He gave his serial number.

The interrogator made a couple more attempts, then said, "You are dismissed, Sergeant."

Earl was escorted to a guardhouse, and pushed through a doorway into a small cell. The door locked behind him.

A guard brought tea. Earl sat on the edge of the hard cot, cup in one hand, cradling ribcage with the other. He took a sip.

"Ach! They must be giving mint tea to prisoners because nobody else will drink it. It's awful!" He thought about his situation, and worked at getting the tea down.

A couple of days passed. He'd be allowed to make a broadcast if he'd say he was being treated well. Feeling this was the case, under the circumstances, and hoping to get word to the folks back home that he was alive, he made the broadcast. Several ham radio operators got the message and sent postcards to his mother, referring to him as Carl Benson, Earl Henson, letting her know he was alive and held prisoner in Germany.

He was sent, with others, to Dulag Luft Transit Camp at Oberursel, Germany, near Frankfurt on the Maine. Dulag Luft, known as The Sweat Box, for inhumane procedures used at times, was an interrogation camp where German intelligence officers made concentrated efforts to gain information.

Earl was brought into a room and handed a so-called Red Cross Form full of questions about the number of planes in the group, details of the mission, and other significant military material. He examined it, put down name, rank, serial number, filled in the part asking his position with Chicago Pimp, then handed the paper back. The interrogator glanced at it, then shoved it back across the desk.

"You must fill this out. It is an important Red Cross form." Earl refused. The officer cursed.

"How will you like to be kept in solitary confinement in your cell for the duration of this war?" Earl glared at him.

"You do what you will. I'm doing what's right." A guard took the uncooperative prisoner back to his cell.

More attempts were made later that day. When asked questions, Earl gave name, rank, and serial number. The interrogators did not like American attitudes.

Earl spent several days in an eight by ten foot cell, alone, unable to see out a small vent window near the ceiling. His wounds were infected, their only attention came from using part of his limited drinking water for cleansing them. Isolated from the crew, since capture, he wondered if they were okay.

Clyde Smith was in a cell next to his. Smitty had made it out of the plane and, now, here he was, yelling obsenities at the guards, and talking to himself most of the time.

Nights were pitch black. The English were bombing Frankfort's marshalling yards. Several times during the long nights, bombs missed intended targets and exploded nearby, shaking the buildings.

"Throw one in here!" hollered Smitty.

Scared, miserable, Earl didn't sleep much. Night after night, mice skittered along the roof of the tiny cell.

"Or are they rats? God, I'm freezing! He shook under the single pressed-fiber blanket. Moving forced broken ribs to grind against each other, pain uneased by the thin mattress.

"Don't you stupid-assed krauts know what a doctor is...?

136

You can't keep us locked up in this stinking hell hole!" He gritted his teeth, and moaned through them.

"Oh, God...! I hurt!"

Pitch-black, cold darkness closed in.... Holding a trembling hand up, he tried, but couldn't see it in front of his face.... Horror captured, then filled his mind.... Gut wrenching realization flooded in, swept forward as if thrust there by a raging river.

"My nightmare...! The dream...! Oh, my God..., This is my dream!" Eyes widened with fear..., then filled with tears. Pressed upon him..., no longer a premonition, the reality was worse than he'd ever dreamed it.

"Oh..., God! No...! Why is this happening? Get me out of here!" Hard fists beat against mattress and wall. "Can't.... be.... here! No...! Why're You making me do this...?"

The air near his head suddenly felt warm. Howard's voice filled his head.

"Never stop praying, brother...." Earl sucked in a breath.

"Howie.... Oh, God, I'm sorry...! Somehow, I gotta deal with this..., I know I do. You kept me alive.... I'm still in one piece.... It's up to me now." He wiped a sleeve across his face.

"Get a grip, Benson! You're not wasting tears on this lousy, stinkin' place. What the hell good would it do, anyway? You can't let it get you! Gotta make.... whatever happens.... as bearable as you can, and get through this." He took a breath, then exhaled slowly.

"Howard..., Red..., Johnny..., Ernie..., they're all out there lookin' for you, right now, so shape up! If God wants it this way, then this is how it's gonna be..., for now." He closed his eyes and whispered into the darkness.

"I'll be home before you know it, guys.... Us Benson boys are tough...."

He was hungry all the time. Once a day, a small portion of rutabaga soup, wormy horsemeat, or boiled potatos and mint tea, was passed into him.

Each morning he was taken to be interrogated. Various agents tried to obtain information, enticing him with better quarters, food, and today, a couple of cigarettes. Earl took a couple of drags on one, stubbed it out, then tucked both into his shirt pocket. The interrogator placed the wrinkled Red Cross form on the desk.

"Sergeant Benson, don't you want to be in the barracks with your crewmembers?" Earl rubbed his chin.

"Sheeeit! What the hell's the difference? I'd still be locked up! Why don't you.... take your lousy paper and shove it where the sun don't shine?" He wadded it, then rolled it across the desk. The agent blinked, then shouted.

"Guard! Take Sergeant Benson back to his cell!"

Over, and over, he was returned to solitary. After several days with no medical attention, his ribs were taped, the process slow and deliberate, by a medical aide, who wrapped wide tape around and around, starting way up under Earl's armpits.

"Wait a minute! What about my hai...oww! Now, hold on, fella! My back and chest..., there's a lot of hai...eeyowww! Take it easy! Fer cryin' out loud!" The medic overlapped the tape all the way down to Earl's bellybutton, then had him returned to his cell.

After so many unsuccessful interrogations, the Germans tired of getting nowhere. They transferred a load of prisoners, including Earl, to a section of camp run by the English Royal Air Force. He was given his first English-American Red Cross Parcel, medical care, and decent food. He made new friends and occasionally saw crewmembers. The officers had been sent to another camp. Separated, assigned to various barracks, Earl and the rest of the crew were isolated from one another.

"Damn good, I'd say..., breakfast, then honest to goodness English tea, lunch, more tea, then supper. Not much in the meals, but with tea in between, I feel like I'm always eating..., so..., when's the other shoe gonna drop?" The respite lasted a couple of weeks.

The other shoe dropped. Men were herded into cattle cars and sent by rail to southeastern West Germany, to Stalag 7-A, near Moosburg. Conditions were deplorable, with about thirty prisoners packed into each car, The trip, of two or three days, made Earl lose track of time, friends, and crewmembers, and he was relieved when they reached their destination.

"KRIEGSGEFANGENENLAGER," he tried saying it..., it being the first thing he saw when he walked into Stalag 7-A. He stared at it.

"If that's just one German word, I'm in trouble. I'll never be able to figure it out."

One after another, men were issued prisoner dog tags. Earl stared at his.

"Stalag VII-A." Below that he read, "112037." New prisoners were ordered to wear the tags about their necks and never remove them.

Earl followed a line of men to an area where they sat on a bench and had their heads shaved. Then, guards ordered them to move to another area, then strip. Their bodies were sprayed, deloused with DDT. After awhile they rinsed in a cold shower.

Earl put his flying coveralls, laden with weeks of filth, back on. He slipped his boots on, then pulled on his warm, fur-collared flying jacket. He was handed a rough blanket made from some kind of pressed fiber.

Assigned to a numbered barracks, he located the building, entered, then chose a bunk. Three tier bunks held twelve men each. Four men slept in each tier, separated by planks about eight inches high. Mattresses, made of thin burlap, were stuffed with straw, bedbugs, lice, mites, and fleas.

It wasn't long before Earl ran out of cigarettes. The warm flying jacket was traded to a Hungarian prisoner for several packs that he stuffed into his coverall pockets.

Prisoners were given their first taste of attack dogs, big, ferocious, German Police dogs, trained to kill on command, set loose by guards, for the fun of watching prisoners scramble into barracks. Several times during air raids, as prisoners stood outside watching, guards, turned dogs loose in the compound. Vicious canines on their heels, prisoners scrambled through doors and windows. Once inside, they bolted to top bunks, where they defended themselves with bed slats. Dogs barreled in and, whap! Men beat them until they'd had enough. Tails tucked between legs, the defeated animals yelped and sprinted from the barracks. Earl saw several men mutilated, throats ripped by the savage beasts. There were survivors of bites to groins, legs, and arms. The guards laughed at their game.

One day, Earl flew through a barracks window and landed against a cement tub. Skinned up, dog right behind, he made it to a top bunk, then helped beat the dog senseless.

It wasn't long before men enticed dogs into the barracks. Once in, doors blocked, bed slats evened odds. Dead dogs were thrown out, and the Americans laughed... at their game.

Several weeks passed. Working gingerly, Earl tried to remove himself from the tape. A German medic spotted him, studied the situation a moment, grabbed the end of the tape and, before Earl could open his mouth, had spun him, several turns, yanking tape, strips of skin, and hair off, as Earl yelped.

"Stupid son-of-a-bitch!" was one expletive Earl used on the aide, who sent him away with nothing for the raw spots.

Earl dabbed a good deal of his daily allotment of water onto the wounds, trying to keep them clean. He shook his head.

"Filthy hell hole!"

The Russians, in their compound, got the same swill the Americans were fed, only less. They weren't laughing or playing games when it came to the malicious, German Police dogs. Dogs were lured into barracks, killed, then eaten.

To get more rations from the Germans, the Russians held up dead and dying comrades, daily, during roll calls, a Russian on each side of a dead or dying man, while the Germans counted heads. Counting finished, prisoners dismissed, they dropped the bodies and re-entered the barracks. Earl watched.

"Unbelievable! Four, five guys, maybe more, laying out there in the mud, just crumpled bodies, most of 'em deader than doornails." Earl noticed that every dead man the Russians carried out for burial had a huge, bloated, pot belly and the rest of him was skin, draped over so many bones.

Typhoid fever from contaminated food and water, and Diptheria, were other diseases that took a heavy toll on camp population. Starvation took most.

The Germans made the Russians bury their own dead, as many died of Typhus after being bitten by infected fleas and vermin. They provided beer so they'd work hard, getting burials done. Being so malnourished, it didn't take much stout, German brew to get the Russians drunk. Earl heard them singing.

"Naz Dhrovia...." He watched them carry dead out on stretchers to the graveyard. The Russians had indomitable spirit, drank the beer, buried their dead..., and were still singing when they came back into camp.

One time, some of their officers were holed up in a barracks. The Germans tried to make them come out to go to work, but the Russians refused. Guards sent a dog in.... The Russians threw its collar out. Another dog.... The prisoners did not throw the collar out. The Germans poured gasoline around the barracks....

"If you do not come out, we are going to burn you out!" Earl and some friends watched a guard light a match.... and..., the Russians marched out, singing boisterously.

"Naz Dhrovia...!" They sang their way out the gate, as guards shook their heads. They were out..., but the Germans had a hell of a time doing it.

Dividing compounds in camp, down the middle, was a narrow street called, International Way.

One day, Earl and some friends watched through the fence as a guard walked by, a huge German Shepherd attached to a short leash beside him. A French prisoner, headed toward the front gate to go out on a work detail, approached. As he passed, the German turned the dog loose with a command to attack.

"Whoa, baby...!" said Earl. The dog barked, growled, then lunged. In a split second, the man clasped the dog's upper and lower jaws, forced them open, twisted its neck in one swift move, flipped it onto its back, then kicked it in the stomach.

"Holy doggynuts! Did'ja see that?" Earl grinned, shook his head, then, whistled. The dog lay still, helpless, dazed, wind knocked out of him. The Frenchman glared at the guard.

"Come get your dog..., or I will kill him." The German picked up the beaten dog, then carried it away. Earl cheered with the others.

A couple days later, the Frenchman, on his way out, met the same guard. As he neared, the dog cowered and moved to the far side of the guard. The guard cursed, and jerked its head up. Earl's group had another good laugh, as the dog rolled onto its back and whimpered..., until its conqueror was gone.

American prisoners were dismayed at the Germans' interpretations of the Geneva Convention. Each rare letter Earl got from home was censored, barely readable, and full of blacked out lines. His letters were cryptic.

"This place reminds me of the beautiful spot on the hill on the right side of the road coming into Unionville. It has a big building, just like it, surrounded by vast green lawns." He had refered to the mausoleum and the cemetery.

Letters from home, were welcome treasures to some, heartbreaking for more than a few, but, a significant number of representations from America brought out hostile anger in many. Earl watched men open letters, only to have a white feather float to the floor..., the sign of a coward.

He listened as a friend read, "How could you desert our country? You are a...." his friend halted, then continued, "a coward for allowing yourself the luxury of sitting on your ass in a safe, healthy, German camp, while decent men are out there fighting and dying to keep America free." Earl did not miss the tear that started down his friend's face.

"D-don't even think about coming home. We never want to see your lousy face again.... Wha....? Oh, Gawwd..., where they gettin' this stuff...? We're talkin' 'bout my family, here!"

Another friend, in Earl's barracks, got a letter from his

girl back in the States that read, "I don't love you any more. You're a quitter and, furthermore..., I'm marrying your father." He didn't finish. It was wadded, then flung into the stove.

Plain and simple, life in this prison camp was miserable existance. Once-per-day meals consisted of a small cup of cabbage soup, dehydrated until mixed with water and boiled. Teeming with well-cooked maggots, the legless larva floated about in the broth and were, at first, spooned out onto the ground. Then Earl saw a good number of prisoners devouring the little white worms. Told it meant valuable protein, mind over matter, and could mean the difference between life and death in a place like this, he stared into his soup....

"Come on, Benson, you gotta do this.... God...! People eat grasshoppers or grubs, but I never...!" He picked up a small, black-mouthed maggot, placed it on the back of his tongue, washed it down with a quick sip of soup, then shivered.

"Eeeughh! Mind over matter, huh?"

Soon, he ate all the nourishing bits. New men watched Earl and friends chew maggots, bite heads off, wiggle bodies between teeth, suck them slowly through lips, and got more than half-sick, which meant more soup for veteran krieges until desperate hunger wore the new arrivals down.

At times, prisoners were given boiled barley or unwashed, unpeeled, boiled potatos. One potato..., for an entire day. New men peeled skins off and discarded them, then stared in disbelief as the sand-specked, dirt-encrusted skins were snatched up, brushed off, and devoured by veteran krieges.

When Red Cross parcels came, things were still difficult. Contents were traded between prisoners for cigarettes or other items. Often, after parcels were distributed, all a prisoner got from the Germans for several days was a single cup of hot water. If he had coffee or a teabag to put in it, he was damn

144

lucky. Some days, all he had was the hot water to get him through the next twenty-four hours until time to eat again.

At times, there was black bread, made with a portion of sawdust, one piece per man. This could be rolled into a small ball of sticky putty. Earl ate his, and watched a guy throw his wadded piece against a wall. It stuck there until someone snatched it off and ate it. The bread was to swell after eaten and make them feel full. Earl never felt full, not even close.

Once in awhile, a horse died, and each barracks got a small piece of wormy meat to cook and divide up. It didn't take long for softies to toughen, once the demand of hunger took over. If one didn't overlook dirt and worms, and learn to make the best of what there was, he didn't survive.

If and when one got a Red Cross parcel, it held Nescafe coffee, small tin of margarine, packages of cheese and crackers, Spam or canned meat, concentrated chocolate D-bar, powdered milk, sea rations, small tin of jam, and cigarettes, Lucky Strikes, Phillip Morris, Wings, or Camels.

Some prisoners used powdered milk, margarine, crackers, and chocolate from parcels, made delicious pies, then traded small pieces for cigarettes or other needs.

Most Red Cross parcels never made it to the prisoners. Out of the four per month one was to have gotten, only one would be given to him. Parcels that got to the prisoners were, most times, minus a good amount. The Germans stockpiled the rest, and always had American cigarettes.

After several escape attempts, the Germans bayoneted all ration cans, upon delivery, forcing immediate consumption. It wasn't long before Earl made a decision.

"Time to get the hell out of here."

CHAPTER
THIRTEEN

A WALK THROUGH FREISING

Earl devised a plan for three men to escape. He chose an English Royal Air Force navigator, Mack, to keep them going the right direction, and an American infantryman, Sonny, to keep them moving, to escape with him. The underground soon knew of their plan, and were to meet them in five days in Munich. They'd be sealed in a boxcar at the train depot, transported to Switzerland, then interned for the duration of the war. The underground knew which cars would be searched, and which trains would go straight through. American ground forces were not in Germany. There'd be nowhere to turn if anything went wrong.

Plan finalized, Earl and his accomplices spent days going out of camp with a work crew. American airmen weren't allowed on work details because they'd been trained in escape and evasion. To get out, Earl got dog tags from an Army infantryman and wore them, when volunteers were checked. He hid his own in a pocket. Each day, he stood near Mack and Sonny, all were chosen, and walked out of the American compound with twenty-seven other prisoners.

Out on International Way, Earl threw the borrowed tags over the fence into the compound, where his benefactor waited. Men in the group distracted the guards, so the toss was unnoticed, and Earl slipped his own tags back on. Daily, the crew dug a prisoner graveyard, and buried food and supplies hidden on their bodies each morning.

It was June, weather right, as thirty men marched out the front gate in ordered columns, three abreast and ten deep. Guards counted as they left early, then returned each afternoon.

Coming in.... was another thing. Thirty prisoners milled about. The guard counted, as half marched in, five or six crouched, duck-walked to the back of the line, outside the gate, then popped up, and re-entered. The guard, confused, disgusted, frustrated as hell, waved the whole mess through.

"Dreisig!" Mack grinned at Earl and Sonny.

"Thirty! Wouldn't you know it, gents?" Earl laughed.

The ritual was performed each day. Three guards, pledged to shoot escapees, followed on bicycles. Most were older, sometimes crippled. They watched the krieges dig graves for dead Americans. During the long days, Earl and his friends gave the guards cigarettes, were friendly, and obeyed each command, hoping to soften attitudes and lessen the chance of being shot while escaping. As days passed, Earl grew excited about the prospect of being free.

The day arrived. Returning to camp, Earl, Mack and Sonny took the lead, three abreast, Earl on the left. Signals stretched the column, as they approached a long, hilly curve. For a few critical seconds it was impossible for the guards to see the first couple rows of men. Off to the right was a good-sized mound of dirt. Sonny, Mack, then Earl bolted for it.

Glancing back, Earl saw a guard, machine gun aimed..., and threw himself behind the mound. Heart thudding in his chest, he peered over at him. Eyes locked in silence....

With a subtle nod, the guard lowered his gun, shrugged, then turned away, shaking his head. Earl ducked as the other guards rode into view.

The trio waited while the column passed, then heard the remaining twenty-seven prisoners singing. Earl wiped his brow.

"Won't be any problems at the gate."

The men hid in a wheat field until dusk, then returned to the cemetery, dug up their knapsacks, and began walking toward Munich, eighty treacherous miles ahead.

Hitler Youth Brown Shirts would look for escapees. Ages about eight to sixteen, they weren't allowed to carry guns until they proved they'd killed an enemy. They had knives, and wouldn't hesitate to slit a throat if they caught a sleeper.

The men knew they couldn't stop at night. They'd hide during the day for a rest, and there'd be one awake and alert to warn of attack. Earl was confident, excited, and exuberant.

"With the start we got, it won't take long to get to Munich. It's sure going to be good in Switzerland, compared to what the Germans put us through." He rubbed a hand over his shrunken stomach. "I'm havin' me the biggest, tenderest, most mouthwatering steak, baked potato with lots of butter, the greenest, sweet peas you ever saw, salad with lots of dressing, and a gigantic, creamy, thick, vanilla milkshake!"

Miles passed. His tongue stuck to the top of his mouth. "Man, I'm thirsty...!"

They came upon a pond. He drank, while Mack and Sonny watched and fought the urge pushing hard at their backsides. Sonny spoke first.

"Damn...! You're crazy, Benson!"

"Yeah," said Mack. "Might be poisoned or unfit." They wouldn't drink, not even when Earl patted his stomach, and assured them he was okay. They backed away, heads shaking.

As they made their way through the town of Freising, Earl could barely see his hand in front of his face. His voice was not a hushed whisper.

"Mack..., you sure you know where we are?"

"Shhh! Yeah, I do. It's Freising, Benson." The

Englishman wore hobnail boots that were now clip-clopping on the brick-paved street. Earl frowned.

"Yeah...? In your navigator mind you think you know right where we're at, but..., something doesn't feel right. Hold up, Mack." He pulled on the airman's sleeve.

"You're absolutely certain this is Freising?" He stopped, then leaned against a pole.

"Man..., I'm beat."

"Clang, clang, claanng...," Mack squatted down.

"Sonny Boy..., would you mind telling the bloke over there that this most certainly is Freising?"

Sonny drew in a breath, then exhaled with a tired yawn.

"Okay. This most certainly is Freising.... What the hell difference does it make, fellas? We're well on our way, here, so let's just cut the crap."

"Claangg, claaanngg, clang...," Earl picked up one foot, then the other, an exercise in futility, to ease painful blisters that had come up on both heels and between a couple of toes.

"Claangg...,"

"That sound.... sure is fam...."

"Cla...," Sudden recognition burned through his mind. He opened his mouth to yell, caught himself..., and whispered.

"Mack, you stupid sonofabitch, I'm gonna kill you!" Mack stood, and scratched his head.

"What the bloody 'ells wrong with you now, Benson?"

"Shhhh! Yeah, Benson," whispered Sonny, "Y' mind keepin' it down?" Earl's fingers fumbled in his pockets, found a match, brought it out..., then struck it against the pole. The match flared. Eyes peered upward as light met with sound.

"God! I don't believe it!" he said through gritted teeth.

"Claaannnnggg!" The clatter of lanyards striking cold metal crashed against his eardrums, sending chills up and down his spine. The flame burned finger and thumb. He dropped it and swore. Sonny's wide eyes met his. They both looked to where Mack stood, hands on hips, ready to defend himself.

"Damn you, Mack! Stupid-assed idiot! Some kinda navigator you are.... Freising my ass! This.... I'll have you know, you dumb limey nincompoop..., is a freakin flag pole..., and we... are smack in the middle of a God-damned German garrison!"

"Blimy, Benson" said the navigator. "You might well be right! Now 'ows about keeping your voice down? Anyway, 'ow in bloody 'ell am I to know if it's the right way and all, with it being so damn bloody black a night out 'ere?"

Quick surmise proved they were..., indeed, in the middle of a military hospital garrison. They got out, undetected.

Earl was exasperated, queasy, and bone-tired.

"You and your stupid directions..., and your stupid boots, clip-cloppin' all over the place..., which by the way, pal, is not Freising, are gonna get our asses killed!"

The threesome walked a ways, then swam a canal to avoid another town. Earl glowered at Mack.

"Sure hope to hell that wasn't Freising, again." He trudged along. "Sheesh! Some kind of navigator.... Ohhh, man...! My stomach!" The pond water was doing a number on his insides. Teeth gritted as cramps made beads of cold sweat stand out on his forehead. He plodded miserably along until dawn. High fever, dysentery, cramps that tied his stomach and intestines into knots, engulfed him.

They rested, settling in some long grass, but, closing their eyes for a moment was a mistake.... as they all fell sound sleep.

"Rat-a-tat...." Earl's eyes flew open. He listened....

"Brrrrrpppp..., Rat-a-tat-tat...." He kicked Sonny, then kicked Mack harder. They sat up, rubbing their eyes.

"Rat-a-tat-tat-tat..., brrrrrrppppp..., zinnnng!"

"Jesus! Get down!"

As daylight allowed their location to be discerned, Earl stuck his head up, then ducked down, flat on his stomach.

"Awh..., crap!" He groaned, rolled onto his back, and threw his arms out. "I don't believe it!" Covering his face with his hands, he rolled onto his stomach, removed his hands, then frowned at Mack and Sonny.

"Gentlemen..., we are damn-near in the middle of a machine gun range. Walking a few steps more last night.... would have put us right in the line of fire." He swore, then held his throbbing head in his hands. "Oh, God..., I feel horrible!" Sonny frowned at Mack.

"I suggest we make like worms and crawl out of here. I also suggest we find a safer place to hide until it gets dark."

The third evening out, they rested in woods near railroad tracks that led to Munich. That's what Mack said, anyway, for what it was worth. They had another town to get through.

Earl drove himself to keep putting one foot in front of the other. Half-way down a moonlit street, he eyed the navigator....

Mack caught the look.

"No, Benson. This isn't Freising, either."

Big as life, twice as ugly, the trio was a grimy, disheveled sight. Earl wore American Air Force flying coveralls, Sonny, an Army uniform, and Mack, a full dress uniform, figuring there'd be no doubt as to who they were if captured. They stood out like three sore thumbs, and that was okay, because, dark as it was, they couldn't see each other's faces let alone uniforms.

Intermittent clouds covered the little moonlight there was. They cut between two buildings, and went up a steep hill to keep from being spotted and keep the right direction.

Three-quarters up, they heard, then saw a soldier

escorting what obviously was a girlfriend, down. Debating whether to run..., they whispered a quick decision. They were committed, it was dark, the German's attention was on the girl. Earl saw he was a sergeant. Sweat made its way into his eyes as they brushed elbows. He smelled peppermint schnapps, cologne, and saw oily, slicked back hair, and a heavy mustache.

"Gut abend," said the jovial sergeant, as he passed.

In his best German, and he prayed it was, Earl replied. Paces quick, they topped the hill, as the man's mind registered.

"Halt..., kreigsgefangenuns! Schweinhunds! Halt!!"

Running full-out, Earl heard Sonny say, "Yes, sir, sergeant, that's what we are... pigdog prisoners, but you ain't catchin' us!" They stopped after a few long minutes, out of breath, listening.

"Must 'ave decided to pursue 'is girl rather then us," said Mack. "All the same, mates, we'd best get far away from 'ere."

Later that night, Earl and Sonny crept into another town. Mack.... did not creep. His hobnail boot heels click-clacked with each step on the cobblestone street. Pitch-black, dim light came from a window here or there. They passed a train station and were temporarily blinded by light when a door flew open.

"Postun?" It was a guard, wanting to know if the noise came from another guard. Earl answered.

"Yah, yah!" The door closed. The group hurried up the street. Upon reaching the outskirts of the town, they heard shouting. Dogs barked. Earl reached into his knapsack.

"You know the plan. Onion on soles, hit it with pepper, throw the dogs off."

"They continued into the countryside, then found railroad tracks and followed them toward Munich.

The fourth night, they were within ten miles of Munich. By daylight, they'd made it into some woods near an antiaircraft detection unit building. Earl was leaving a trail.

"If anyone's followed us, they'll have no problem...." Head pounded, rubbery legs refused to walk straight, and he was on the verge of fainting. Waves of nausea doubled him, but there was nothing left to heave. He collapsed against a tree.

"Can't go on. I'll die...., cause us all to be caught." He slapped his hands back against the trunk.

"Damn it! Why'd I let myself get into this mess? God, we're so close, but I'm a damn fool if I don't know when I'm whipped and..., I am, that's the plain, simple, son-of-a-bitchin' truth.... If I hadn't been so bullheaded and cocky, we'd be in Munich tonight, the underground would be taking care of us. Damn...! Damn it all to hell!" He wiped sweat from his face.

"Gotta.... turn myself in..., get medical help. Ain't no other way. Mack..., Sonny..., you gotta go on without me."

He slumped to his haunches, about to be on his own in this strange, enemy-infested land. Dispair and sickness encompassed him. Tears dampened his eyes. The gunner pounded the tree.

"Knock it off, Benson..., you're not lettin' go! "You're not!" He blinked back the tears, then gave himself orders.

"You will not waste one lousy tear on this. You won't! Your body needs every drop.... damn it! You know what you have to do..., now do it!" Mack and Sonny stared down at him.

Earl raised his eyes to meet theirs.

"Not gonna make it, guys.... You gotta get to Munich on time. I'm holding you up..., can't make it if you have to carry me. Take my knapsack..., there's cigarettes, compass, too..., so you won't get lost, Mack..." He forced a half-grin onto his face.

"Good luck, don't forget to send me a postcard." Strength gathered from somewhere deep inside, he stood, turned his back on them, and stumbled away.

154

I JUST TURNED TWENTY-ONE

Leaving the others deep in the woods, Earl stumbled along the road until he met a German from the spotter station. In what little German he knew, he told the man he'd escaped, was sick, and needed medical aide. He was escorted to a German officer at the detection building. An English-speaking officer was summoned. He checked Earl's dog tags.

"You are hungry?" Earl nodded as the floor swayed.

"Yeah, but..., I'm really sick." The officer took his arm.

"Come with me."

He took Earl to a nearby pub where a buxom, blonde waitress brought steins of ale and a bowl of potato soup to their table. Earl took a sip of ale. The soup smelled delicious. Two mouthfuls went down, then came back up. Doubled over, he choked, and gasped. Horrible retching brought inadvertant tears. Holding the back of the chair with one hand, he grasped the edge of the table with the other, looked miserably and apologetically up at the officer, then, unable to keep him in focus, turned and put both elbows on the table.

"Can't you see I'm sick?" He wiped his eyes, then held his throbbing head in both hands.

Cursing, the waitress stormed over with mop and bucket, then dropped them. Dirty water splashed onto Earl's pant legs. He watched the officer's face as the woman ranted and raved. Wiping cold sweat from his brow, Earl mumbled to himself.

"She's..., she's saying.... I should mop the floor? That's

good..., that's.... real.... good. The officer spoke curtly. The woman shut her mouth. Scowl darker than thunderclouds, she picked up the mop.

The officer stood, then indicated the doorway with an outstretched hand. Earl struggled to his feet, then forced himself to walk out. The waitress swore as he stumbled away.

At the installation's hospital, a doctor examined and weighed him. Earl looked up, saw his head shake, forehead fraught with wrinkles.

"Eighty pounds! You should be dead of exposure! You will stay here. This medicine will help. Take some now." Earl swallowed a mouthful.... It stayed down. The doctor pushed the bottle into Earl's hand.

"Take this each day."

Earl was under his care two days, then guards half-carried him to a cell block, a prison where they kept their own offenders, soldiers who went AWOL, committed crimes or disobeyed orders. His cell door opened into a compound surrounded by eight foot walls, topped with glass. The guards eased him onto a cot, and didn't bother to shut the cell door when they left. Earl tried, but couldn't raise his head.

"Eighty pounds..., lost sixty, since shot down..., three months..., lifetime ago..., unending..., torturous life..time..., of hell...." Pulled into darkness, he fought, afraid to sleep, too scared to let go, as the long night passed.

"Two days..., three...?" He lay listless on the hard cot. "Face.., blur.., hand unh...head..., taste..., med..cine.., water...."

"Three... days...?" Cognizant, flat on his back, he fought to raise his head, forced himself to hold it up for the count of two, then collapsed. "Don't know if... gonna shake this..., gotta find strength..., get out of this...." Hands became fists, pushing against the thin mattress. He issued orders.

"Move.... your.... ass, Ben..s.son!" Veins and sweat stood out on his temples. "One.., two...., three." His head flopped back onto the hard mattress. He prayed.

"God, I promise..., I'll try to be the best person I can be..., if You'll just... get me through this. I'm in your hands." That night he lay on his side and, letting go, slept the night.

The next morning, he pushed himself up on one elbow.

"I'm a mess..., smell like hell..." Fingers combed through scraggly hair, then over chin and upper lip, which were covered with beard and mustache. "Must look like I just crawled out of some prehistoric cave."

As he lay on the vermin-infested bed, German prisoners came to stand outside his cell. They tried to talk to him.

"American?" Earl's answer was weak.

"Yah...." From a distance, a voice hollered.

"Chicago?"

"Yah...., Chicago." Several men relayed the response. A flood of one-word questions came. Earl pointed to himself and forced a half-grin.

"Chicago.... gangster." This was repeated to anyone who listened. They wanted to see the strange American gangster.

In a couple of days, a guard arrived to take the escaped kriege back to 7-A. During the long train ride, his attention was diverted most of the time by female passengers.

Earl sat on the hard seat, weaker than a whipped pup.

Bastard's disgusting. It'd be easy to jump out the window. He pictured it in his mind. I could catch up with the underground in Munich.... Dogged determination made him sit up and gather himself. Sweat broke out on his brow. Commands issued ignored, he slumped back, exhausted, head rocking back and forth..., matching the rhythmicity of the train's wheels on the tracks.

"You're in trouble... you're in trouble... you're in trouble..." He reached into his pocket, brought out the medicine, uncapped it, and brought it to his lips.

Ughh... horrible stuff.... Least I'm doing.... a little better. He slumped onto the seat, curled into a ball, and closed his eyes.

At Stalag 7-A, he was put in a cell with a Polish prisoner. A Red Cross parcel was brought in by a guard. Earl tried to eat, but, unable to hold anything down, gave most of it to his cell mate, who'd been sentenced to life for fraternizing with a German girl. Earl stuffed packs of cigarettes into his pockets.

He took the medicine daily, forced himself to eat, and drank small amounts of water, often, to keep his stomach working. Each time he started to think he might even begin to be able to, he made himself stand and take steps. He counted and added a step each time, driving himself.

"Do it..., or die, Benson! You are going to do this." Teeth ground together in his skeletonized face. The shaky effort to remain on his feet became only somewhat easier.

Over and over, he repeated, "Come on..., you can do it.... Us Benson boys are tough..., damn tough."

Within a week, he was in the commandant's office, facing the camp's first court-martial of an American airman. The stern, beefy-faced commandant spoke through an interpreter.

"Tell me, Sergeant Benson, how did you escape from my camp?" The distance walked from cell to here had left Earl feeling faint. He steadied himself, then looked at the interpreter.

"It was easy..., I walked out the main gate." Learning the meaning of Earl's response, the commandant pounded the desktop with a brawny fist.

"I do not believe you!" He looked Earl in the eye.

"You will tell me, now, Sergeant, how you escaped from this camp!" Earl scowled into his eyes, then answered.

"Well..., it seemed like the proper thing to do..., at the moment..., so I took a leisurely stroll out your front gate." He watched the interpreter's face redden as he translated. The commandant's fist crashed down again.

"Nein! Nein! Du schwein! You will give me the truth!"

Fighting to stay upright, jawline rock hard, Earl's eyes shot fire at the commanding officer, then at the red-faced interpreter. His voice, colder than his mother's had ever been, filled the room.

"I really hate being called a liar. I.... do.... not.... lie...! What I told you is God's truth.... I took a freakin' flyin' leap, and landed outside your freakin' front door!"

Hearing the translation, the commandant was silent, eyes locked on Earl's. The room was quiet, except for a couple of totally ignored, persistent flys that buzzed about and landed on the prisoner's filth-laden flesh and clothing. Hard eyes..., eyes full of death, destruction, hunger, and pain, refused to back down from the commandant's cold stare. The officer blinked, then averted his eyes.

"Dummkopf.... Jetzt wird's mir zu." He said more, then left the room. The words were repeated by the interpreter.

"Blockhead. Now, I have had enough. You will not play these games with me. I sentence you to seventy days of solitary confinement."

Out of the office, on his way to certain death, Earl knew he had to do something. He'd been too ill to smoke. Pockets bulged with cigarettes. Near solitary, he baited the guard.

"Cigarettes..., American. One pack." He pointed at a nearby building.

"Hospital." He stopped, then pointed at himself.

"Me hospital." The guard shook his head, turned Earl around, and nudged him hard in the back. Earl took a step, stopped, indicated the hospital, and took two more packs out.

"Three American cigarettes." Eyes pleading, offer extended, he faced the guard.

"Nein!" Earl was turned, then pushed. At death's door, he took a few steps, halted, faced the guard and, with tear-filled eyes, hands trembling, held five packs of cigarettes out. The guard hesitated, then, with a heavy sigh, took the bribe.

In the hospital, an English doctor examined him while the guard stood near. Earl didn't speak, but stared into the doctor's eyes, filling him with his desperation and misery. The doctor leaned over and looked into Earl's ear.

"Not to worry," he whispered. "You're not going anywhere." He ordered the guard to leave. The guard protested. The doctor won out.

Earl spent sixteen days in his care, until the physician told him he wouldn't be allowed to keep him longer. Beds were needed for the seriously ill and injured. Earl prepared to leave.

"Well, at least I'm off the critical list. He'd gotten a Red Cross parcel, and packed all he could into his coveralls, which had been taken out and washed by a nurse. A different guard escorted him toward solitary. Earl stumbled along.

Can't let him put me in that hell hole..., won't survive..., Worked with the other guard.... Out came a pack of smokes. He stopped and pointed toward the barracks.

"One American cigarettes." Eyes drove deep into the German's. The second pack softened the guard, who shook his head, then pushed Earl toward his barracks. Earl said a silent prayer of thanks.

"Man, oh, man. Never thought.... I'd owe my life.... to a few packs of smokes."

At the barracks, he clutched the door frame, shaking, trying to catch his breath. Inside, men stared.

"Oh..., my.... God...! Benson..., is it you?" Earl let go, knees buckling, and stumbled to his bunk. Unable to climb up, he collapsed onto the bottom one.

"Oh, man! He's in bad shape!" Earl didn't know who said what, then, as everyone crowded about.

"What the hell happened? Where's he been?" Earl looked up into their faces, and swallowed hard.

"Didn't.... make it, guys." Questions flew, about his escape, and whether he'd been in solitary. Earl told a little of what had happened, outside, his return, and how he had bribed the guards. He looked around the group.

"Anyone heard if Mack and Sonny got to Switzerland?"

"That's the two sent to solitary two weeks ago, or so. Hell, they got nabbed in Munich after curfew. You know how conscript laborers work for the Germans and everyone's gotta be off the streets by a certain time because the police are always patroling?" Earl nodded.

"Well, someone said they got lost trying to find the railroad station." Earl closed his eyes.

"How long?" Two men spoke in unison.

"How long what?" Biting hard on his lower lip, Earl finished the question.

"How long will they be in solitary?" He opened his eyes and peered around the group for an answer. It came, and he knew it before it was spoken. He threw an arm over his eyes.

"C'mon, Benson, it's not your fault."

In the days ahead, Earl worried about Mack and Sonny, asking how they looked when brought back, and whether anyone had seen or heard anything more.

"I did the right thing, leaving them in the woods..., wasn't my fault they got lost. Mack couldn'ta found his way out of a wet paper bag, anyway and, from what I've heard, they look a hell of a lot better than me."

"Look, Rascal, there ain't nothing we can do about them, but there's definitely something we can do for you."

Ignoring their own hunger, friends fed Earl cheese and crackers from their Red Cross Parcels to bind him up. The diarrhea was soon controlled, and he was on his feet again.

Mack and Sonny, were out of solitary, covered, head to toe, with lice, flea, and other bug bites, not one square inch of their bodies untouched. They'd made it. Earl, Mack, and Sonny had survived. More prisoners used Earl's plan.

Escapes were successful, especially after he emphasized, "Don't drink pond water!" He had hopes of escaping again, as soon as he was fit enough. He kept busy, building himself up, walking around the compound every day. Some prisoners had made barbells from flattened cans and bars, and Earl lifted weights dilligently. The bellygunner overheard remarks.

"Rascal's the skinniest little turd that ever came chuting from a turret," and, "Yeah, he's got the biggest chest I ever saw on a small guy. Wonder what he'd be like if he ate regular?"

But there was never enough food. When Red Cross parcels came, the Germans gave the American prisoners their usual allotment of soup, as they were supposed to, so there were times when the Americans traded it to the Russians.

In darkness, Russians came over the eight foot fence that separated the compounds. The fence, reinforced with several strands of barbed wire, was topped with coiled barbed wire. There were warning wires, about thirty feet out from each side, running a couple of feet above ground. Russian prisoners came over, or under the wires, over the fence, and strolled into the American compound, to trade goods strapped to their bodies.

Each man took two buckets of swill then, off they went, hopping the warning wire on the American side, walking up one side of the barbed fence, back down the other, then, straddling the warning wire on the Russian side. The entire procedure was performed in seconds without spilling a drop or touching the fences with anything but their feet. Earl had never seen the likes of it and watched, amazed.

"Man, they're fast. I couldn't do it if I used both hands, a rope, and ladder. Sheesh, they could be a circus act!"

Italian prisoners were another matter, and Earl and his friends enjoyed dealing with them. Cigarettes and other items were traded for the cash. Some Italians had lots of American money. Earl was told they'd taken it off of dead soldiers.

One day, Earl watched a friend deal with an Italian trader.

"I want ten of these for this pack of cigarettes." He held up ten fingers, then pointed at the man's one dollar bills, spread out in front of him along with fives, tens, and twenties. The Italian didn't know values of individual bills and wouldn't trade. The American pointed at the man's spread of cash again.

"Okay, I'll take three of these, instead." The Italian happily handed over three ten dollar bills.

One evening, Earl stood near the fence, visiting with a couple of Punjab Indians who knew a few words of English. He'd heard they always wore turbans and never cut their hair because of firm religious beliefs. He knew they braided their beards, then tucked neatly folded paper money under their chins where it couldn't be seen. They never smoked and, they never used toilet paper. Instead, they carried a small bowl of water with them into the toilet, and washed themselves each time. He couldn't understand the waste of good water.

The two Indians on the other side of the fence indicated they wanted him to come into their compound. Earl didn't understand a word, as they spoke their own language now, but they were soft-spoken and friendly. Curious, he watched for a

163

chance, sneaked over, then followed them to a barracks, and discovered he'd be attending a religious service.

He was hatless, so a man brought out a folded turban cloth, about twelve feet long, and wrapped it around Earl's head. When finished, he wore a perfect turban, had been nicknamed 'The Little Maharajah,' and was seated with the rest of the worshipers. A man rang bells attached to a long steel bar, and soon the congregation was chanting. Earl closed his eyes and listened to the soothing sounds. After the service..., curry sauce. He tasted it; winced.

"Not in a million years!" Pudding, made of D-bars, canned milk, and other acquired ingredients came next, and it was good. Earl learned some Punjab words and returned often to visit and attend services.

Punjabs were excellent wrestlers. Matches that reminded Earl of a small version of the Olympics were held between compounds. Guards and officers watched and bet on them. New prisoners, big, tough Americans, were no match for the small, wiry Punjabs, and were pinned in no time.

The roughest bunch in camp were Gurkha Indians, famous as soldiers. Guards wouldn't venture into Gurkha barracks. Earl had heard of a British general in Africa who stood before several hundred German prisoners asking questions. One prisoner with a gun hidden on himself made a move to assassinate the general. Before he could aim, his throat was slit by a Gurkha guard.

Gurkhas fighting for the British moved faster than greased lightning and carried razor-sharp, curved knives. They were paid for bringing an ear back from each slain enemy soldier. British officers made the mistake of not designating which ear, so the Indians sliced both off and got double pay. The British were quick to specify just which ear they'd pay for.

Stalag 7-A was full of interesting people from many places, and Earl learned a great deal. Talk of escapes intrigued him, as he wanted to escape again. The Germans were fed up with continual breakouts, and took control of the situation.

In the fall of 1943, after Earl had been a prisoner almost six months, approximately five hundred American airmen from Stalag 7-A were loaded into railroad cattle cars. Guards herded about fifty men into each car, and locked them in.

"Where we going?" Earl heard the question too many times during the next five days on the rails. Some nights, they were left on side tracks in marshalling yards. The cars shook and rumbled when British bombs exploded nearby.

Once a day, a bucket of wormy rutabaga or cabbage swill was passed in, sometimes with small bits of minced horsemeat in it. Fifty men took turns scooping it out with their hands.

Prisoners were let out of the cars once a day to relieve themselves. Earl tried to be last out and one of the first back in, to avoid stepping into someone else's business. Outside, he stretched and flexed cramped muscles.

"Not that I give a damn, but, what an awful sight and rotton stench for the locals to see and get a whiff of! Five hundred of us, most with the runs, squatted down, baring it all in front of God and everybody.... Well, it's better than the corner some are using in that cattle hauler. Freakin' krauts didn't clean the stinkin' cow shit off the planks. Least they could've thrown a bale of bedding straw into each car. What a mess! Lots of guys are too sick to make it to the corner."

Early morning, the fifth day, Earl watched guards carry more dead away. Several men had lost their final battle in his car alone. Guards ordered the prisoners back inside.

Cold, relentless wind blew through the cars as the train picked up speed. Earl sat as far from the sides as possible.

"Think about the positive end of it.... At least we're not being pestered by flys or mosquitos."

No one spoke unless necessary. Talking hurt. Men had sores in their mouths; parched lips cracked and bled with little or no provocation. It was an extremely difficult and bitter time. Earl sat, cramped, arms wrapped about his knees.

This small space..., it's my whole world..., my entire existance. God..., I can understand if my guardian angel's not here..., hell, who'd want to be..., but I need You.... I can't.... I just can't take much more. I don't understand how anyone can do this to another human! Sure as hell ain't right. No room to move..., filthy, freezing..., starving.... He coughed.

No...! Think positive thoughts, Benson. Okay..., they gotta be taking us to a different camp. They're not killing us, or they'd have done it already. Done it already. Done it already. Oh..., God! I'll never ride on another train, even if my life depends on it! Hell, I don't even want a stupid toy train on a stupid, clickity-clack track!

Face buried in arms, forehead resting on knees, his shoulders heaved with prayer. God..., I need You..., we need You, to keep us. Our days and nights are filled with suffering and dying.... Look at us! No room to lie down. Pain racks our bodies. Hunger eats at our stomachs.... I've seen nothin' but misery, day after day..., chiseled faces of young men, turned old..., hear their moans..., their crys..., watch 'em die...!

He clamped his arms around his head. I just want to shut my eyes..., and wish for blindness..., close my ears and wish for deafness. It's too much..., and the pain...! Oh, God, their pain..., it won't stop until they're.... dead..., and it's too much...! Please, God...! I can't help them..., and it's tearing right through me! Earl sucked in a shuddering breath, then slowly exhaled.

All I wanna do..., is go home..., and be free to walk down

166

the streets of Unionville..., with the sun.... shining down on me.... A tear fell. He caught himself.

No! Think positive thoughts! Don't let go.... It ain't over yet. Be strong...., live for today...., and tomorrow. His face grew warm, then hot, fingernails dug into scalp.

Oh..., hell, Lord! I just turned twenty-one! Never loved life much..., 'til now.... Fists clenched. Now..., I have nothing..., don't know where they're taking us, or what's gonna happen from this moment on..... Jaws clamped, teeth ground.

Plain and simple, Lord, You're my salvation, I'm in Your hands. Biting hard on the inside of a cheek, he tasted blood.

I know I said this before, but I need to say it again.... I need You to hear me! I promise..., no..., I swear..., if You'll just give me the strength.... to get through this..., and help me make it home..., I'll be the best kind of person I can possibly be.... just help me.... find a way!

From somewhere across the dim lit car, someone began to sing, voice bold, parched, and dry, but incredibly good. More voices picked it up.

Cold shivers shot along Earl's spine as he realized what it was. He raised his head.... Tears streamed down his face.

God was answering his prayer, in an unquestionable way, because anyone who could sing, did so. Earl joined in.

"God bless America.... land that I love.... Stand beside her.... and guide her.... through the night with the light from above.... From the mountains.... to the prairies.... to the oceans.... white with foam. God bless America...., my home..., sweet.... home!"

The train stopped at Krems, Austria.

Most of the prisoners stepped down from the cattle cars, but many were carried out. Earl climbed down and looked around the depot. A few civilian passengers, neatly dressed ladies and gentlemen, stood on the platform. When they saw prisoners urgently dropping their pants, and smelled the horrific odor of feces and the stench of vomit from the cattle cars and men, they covered their noses, and turned away in disgust.

The prisoners were not welcome here. The filthy Americans were spat upon and cursed by passersby while being unloaded, and during their five mile force march up the road.

CHAPTER FIFTEEN

CATS HAVE NINE LIVES

Stalag XVII-B. Earl's eyes took it in. Cold, wrapped in barbed wire, atop a barren hill, surrounded by precisely placed guard towers, this was one hell of a lonely, well-secured place. Surrounding land had been cleared for quite some distance, the entire area devoid of trees and brush for at least two hundred yards. Once through the main gate, he heard dogs barking.

"Those aren't Shepards," he said to a tall man standing next to him. Ahead of them, prisoners laughed and pointed. The man peered over to where the yip, yip, yips came from, then looked down at Earl.

"They're Spitz. Heard of them being used in other camps. Little bastards are trained to bark their butts off if someone tries to escape." As the line pressed forward, Earl spotted the dogs jumping about on their leashes, and laughed.

"Can't do much, but bark. Shoot, those little buggers can't hurt us.... We'd just grab a tail, and throw 'em!"

Starving, filthy, uncomfortable as hell, prisoners were put through the delousing procedure, rinsed, and allowed to climb back into their filthy, vermin infested clothing again. One after another, they were given blankets and assigned barracks. Earl was sent to barracks 29-B. He looked around.

"Home, sweet hell hole." Midway in, he threw his thin pressed-fiber blanket on an upper bunk, claiming the high spot.

"Winter's coming. Don't wanna be near the doors. Cold air goes down. Warm air, if there's ever such a thing in these places, goes up. Dogs are small, but could reach lower bunks with their sharp little teeth. No thanks."

Eventually, 29-B with nearly a hundred and sixty-nine men crowded into it, had a barracks chief named Tom Bagwell. Chow king was Eli Rogers, and Vernon Williams was in charge of Red Cross parcels and clothing.

Earl wandered about and discovered Bill Hovekamp in barracks 35-A, and Clyde Smith in 37-A. The environment was much the same as Stalag VII-A, camp split down the middle with an International Way, Russians still holding up their dead during daily roll calls. XVII-B was escape proof, according to the Germans. Krieges could not escape. Not from up here. Trip wires, trenches, mines and guards kept prisoners in.

But, some prisoners dug tunnels. One group burrowed two weeks, miscalculated, and came up between the two fences where guards walked the perimeter. The hole, discovered when a guard making rounds darn-near fell in, was investigated to determine its origin. Guilty parties were rounded up. Earl and others watched as the offenders were marched at gunpoint out to the hole, handed shovels, then told to fill it in.

One crafty culprit said, "We can't start here. We've got to cover it up from the inside, and work our way outward. We can't just cover up this end, because then the hole would still be open from here into the barracks." The fun started. The perpetrators were allowed to re-enter the hole between the fences. They went through the tunnel, back into the barracks, where they laughed themselves silly, then, wiping smiles from their faces, marched from the barracks to the warning wire, near where the guards waited. Bold and daring, they mimicked the guards by standing, feet spread, hands clasped behind backs, rocking back and forth on the balls of their feet while the guards watched the hole, waiting for the prisoners to come out. The real fun came when, in German, one of the cat-and-mouse team members asked a guard what was going on, and the excited guard explained that a great number of Americans were caught trying to escape.

A second member of the almost-made-its asked where the fliegen gangsters had gone to. The guard stared at the hole. Consternation, like the turn of a red-hot screw, twisted his facial features. The Germans had not only lost the entire group, but were now unable to remember who the guilty parties were. The wanna-be-escapees' quick wits, ingenuity and senses of humor managed to bring them through the ordeal unscathed.

In his barracks, Earl shook his head as he watched a radio being hidden in a wall.

"I've seen about everything in this camp. Only thing I haven't seen made from cans is a gun. Saws, knives, eating utensils, barbells; amazing what comes of a few pieces of tin."

He worked out with barbells, as did numbers of men, realizing he had to make the effort. Some didn't, got soft and died, and some went crazy. A friend, Dave, kept saying he was going over the fence. Earl grabbed his sleeve.

"That's suicide, man.... They'll kill you! Hang on a little longer, guy. This ain't gonna last. We'll be home, eating steak and eggs before you know it."

Several nights later, gunfire erupted out in the yard. Earl was first to reach the doorway. He stared at the fence. Mortally wounded, in agony, illuminated by a spotlight, Dave hung, tangled in coiled barbed wire near the top. He reached out, and screamed.

"Benson! Help me! Oh..., God!" Earl's heart pounded in his ears. A voice..., he didn't realize was his own, screamed.

"Nooooo!" He stepped from the shadowy darkness of the barracks doorway. Midstride, he was grabbed from behind, lifted off his feet and hauled back into the barracks.

"Lemme go, ya stupid son-of-a-bitch!" He struggled. A hand clapped over his mouth.

"You can't help him!" It was Gene, a bunkmate. He toted Earl back to the bunk, threw him up onto it, crawled in, then laid a firm hand on Earl's arm.

"Go back to sleep."

Earl finally closed his eyes, but the horrific image of his friend was there..., painted on the backs of his eyelids.

He fought to blot it out, but, into the early morning hours, heard, over and over, "Bensonnnn! Please...., help meeee! Oh, Gaawwwd!" Each time..., he sat bolt upright, eyes filled with tears, clenched fists twisted and pressed against his temples.

"Can't go out!" said Gene. "If the bastard ever cared about anything beyond his own miserable son-of-a-bitchin' self, he wouldn't be out there right now, putting you, me, and everyone else in this frickin' place through this hell!"

The horror of losing a good friend was forced to hide in the back of his mind as Earl spent most of his time working out. Hands became hard, calloused. A blister formed across the web between the two middle fingers of his left hand, broke and, in a few days, the hand was infected. Within hours, he couldn't see between the fingers, and his arm was swollen. Red streaks ran to his armpit, and he felt a hard kernal there.

At the infirmary, he was weighed.

"Eighty-two pounds? Damn, I'm light in the shoes again today!" he told the assistant.

An American doctor, an infantryman, looked at the hand, brow furrowed.

"Blood poisoning, Sergeant.... I'll have to cut it open."

Earl's eyes widened.

"Got anything you can give me for pain?"

"No..., nothing like that here."

"You mean you're just gonna cut it?"

"Sergeant, you're about forty-eight hours away from experiencing your own death. You won't feel this."

Earl smirked.

"Well, which is it, Doc? I won't feel the cut, or my own death?" One eyebrow shot up. The doctor almost smiled.

"Hopefully neither. Get up on the table." Earl eyed it.

Never make it, not one-handed. The doctor caught the look, picked him up, sat him on the table, dipped the swollen hand in a bucket of iodine, then, scalpel in hand, sliced between Earl's fingers, laying the palm wide open.

Pus spurted, then pus and blood poured from the wound. Placing both hands under Earl's armpit, the doctor milked the poison down the arm several times. Earl grimaced.

"Thought you said I wouldn't feel it!"

"One out of two's not bad," said the doctor. "Least you won't feel your death now." He worked along the arm until satisfied he'd extracted as much poison as possible. Nauseous, light-headed, Earl swayed forward, but caught himself.

"Whoa.... Hope I don't pass out or toss the cookies!" He stiffened his backbone, and took deep breaths as the wound was coated with sulfanilimide powder, then wrapped in bandages. The doctor handed over two pills and a cup of water.

"That wasn't so bad." Earl downed the pills.

"Maybe not for you, but for me.., it was excruciating."

That night, he stayed in the infirmary. In the morning, he waited in the examination room. The doctor strolled in, grabbed him, and plunked him onto the table.

"Let's see it, Benson. How's it doing?" He unwrapped the bandages, took the hand into his own, turning palm upward.

"Hmmm..., doesn't look too bad. Hold it out here where

I can get a good look at it." Earl pushed the hand forward.

Whamm! The fist slammed into Earl's palm, breaking the incision wide open. Earl swore, and jumped from the table.

"Damn! What'dja go and do that for? Man..., oh, man.... that hurt!" Ignoring the protest, the doctor picked his patient up and set him back onto the examination table. Earl glared at him.

"Been doing any skunk huntin' lately?" The doctor reached under Earl's armpit.

"That's a strange question.... Never have, probably never will. Why?" His firm hands worked down the arm.

"Just.... ohhh..., God..., thought I'd ask!" Earl held his forehead with his good hand, and looked away. "Oh, Jesus...! When will it ever end?" The arm was milked, powdered, then wrapped in fresh bandages. Earl was told to return to barracks, then report back each day for four or five days, at least, so the doctor could keep an eye on his condition. Earl frowned.

One more night in a clean bed under clean sheets and a couple of blankets, with a little more food would've been nice.

Each day, the doctor found a new way to trick him into exposing his hand for the painful method of cure. On the last day, Earl sat in a chair by the doctor's desk.... glaring at him.

"You ain't touchin' my damn hand."

"Well then, just lay it over there on my desk so I can at least see how it's doing." He looked Earl straight in the eyes, hands raised in surrender.

"I won't touch it." Earl laid his hand on the desk. The doctor glanced out through the doorway, and did a double take.

"Whoa, sweet baby! Where the devil did she come from?" Earl looked.

Bammm! Earl jumped up, grabbed him by the front of his uniform, and shrieked.

"Stupid son-of-a-bitchin' bastard! Hit me again, and I'll....

Strong hands forced Earl's arms down. Cold, hard eyes drove into his. The doctor set him down hard on the chair.

"I'm saving your miserable life, Benson...! I'll do whatever it takes to keep you, or any other man who walks in here, alive." He reached up under Earl's arm, and was not gentle about it. The arm was milked, medicated, dressed and, then, a guard escorted Earl back to his barracks. The hand healed, and Earl went right back to lifting weights.

Winter came, too soon, and he couldn't believe how cold it got. Most days, prisoners did only what they had to do. The rest of their time was spent trying to stay warm.

Shivering in bed, blanket up to chin, Earl looked outside.

"Damn, it's cold!" Long, woolen underwear hung over a line outside the barracks next door. He leapt from the bunk, ran out, snatched them, ran inside, yanked off his pants, slipped into the underwear, tugged his pants back on, climbed into the bunk, rolled up in the blanket, and luxuriated in the additional warmth.

"Ahhh! This is more like it. Think I'll take a little nap." He closed his eyes.

"What...? What the hell? Something's biting me! He slapped at the burning, itching spot. "Owww.... damn!"

Someone must've rang a dinner bell, for he scratched, slapped, fidgeted, then scratched some more.

"Hell! I can't take anymore of this!" He scrambled from the bunk, out of his pants, out of the long johns and, taking a close look, found the source of his misery.

"Crime a Nellie...! They're loaded!"

Outside, shivering in frigid air, he hung them on the line.

"S-some idiot put these b-babies out here hoping to freeze the lice to d-death. Well..., lotsa luck, fella! Wonder how many t-times your woolie undies will disappear and reappear today? B-bet you're watching the whole show, and think it's funny....

175

Well, har-dee-harrrr..., and more p-power to ya!"

December, 1943, forty degrees below zero, it was decided the krieges must be deloused. The prisoners were freezing and, learning the Germans' intentions, taking matters into their own hands..., something they did on a regular basis, anyway..., rubbed margarine mixed with sand into their hair.

The enthusiastic detail sprayed everything and everyone in the barracks with DDT. When time to shave heads, bigger, healthier men took a seat on the bench. Clippers buzzed through the first and second job, but the sand did as intended.

"Clunk. Zip. Clunk!" Three heads shaved.

"Zip. Clunk. Thud!" Fit to be tied, blades useless, the detail packed their gear, then left the barracks.

Men who'd sacrificed stood out from the rest, as lost locks regrew. They wrapped cloths about their necks and heads, and pulled hats down over their ears.

Things continued to deteriorate. Going out to the toilet, a very large forty-hole version of the two-holer Earl had grown up with, was to go in harms way. Hinged sections of seats were lined up over a huge pit that was emptied only when ready to overflow. Several prisoners were bitten by rats. Men looked, if they dared sit, then kept eyes focused down between their legs.

Work details were assigned to fill honeywagons with waste, then teams of horses pulled the wagons out of camp.

Earl watched prisoners stir up guards one day before a load of waste was taken out. To distract them, a couple of men lured the guards with conversation and cigarettes, then showed them nudes someone had drawn. Two men meandered over, loosened lug nuts on a wheel of the wagon, then vanished into a crowd of prisoners headed to the front gate. The wagon reached the congested area, the wheel fell off, the load splattered across the roadway, and guards and officers stepped around the mess, swearing and holding their noses. Earl laughed with friends.

"Just the way we like it!"

One day, he sat in the barracks reading a book that was being passed around. The roll call order had been given, but, engrossed in the story's climax, he continued down the page. A guard stormed over.

"Raus!" Earl ignored him.

"Ausrollen!" Earl glanced up.

"Keep your pants on. I'm coming...."

Whamm! Rifle butt slammed into the left side of his face, knocking him to the floor. The book landed at the guard's feet. He booted it under a bunk, raised the rifle, and shouted.

"Raus! Schweinhund!" Earl eyes never left the guard. He rolled, sprang to his feet as the gun butt missed and slammed against the floor, and shouted as he ran from the barracks.

"Dickhead Nincompoop!" He disappeared among the men in the yard. As they assembled for the count, he touched his jaw, felt it swelling in the frigid air, and swore. After roll call, he went to the infirmary.

"Broken," said the doctor.

"Hurts...!"

"Yes."

"So...?"

"So keep it shut..., and make it out to roll calls on time."

Prior to Christmas, 1943, potatoes were distributed to the barracks. By adding raisins and sugar, a brew was fermented into wine. Some distilled their's into white lightnin'. A couple men overindulged and died.

Christmas eve, Earl and a few friends got snockered and decided to celebrate outside between the barracks. A rock was hurled at a guard tower.

"Sheeshhh, you cun do butter in nat," said a reveler.

Rocks and stones flew through the air, and thudded against the sides of the tower. Earl picked up a good-sized stone, took aim, and zinged it into the tower. It ricocheted, bounced back, and stung the guard, who yelled, ducked, then shined his spotlight in their direction.

"Way to go, Rascal!" someone whispered. Things were quiet until the light went out. Earl zinged another rock into the tower. "Merry Christmas, ya Nazi bastard," he yelled. "Yer too stupid to win a war!" He stumbled back into the barracks.

"Think I'll catch some of the Christmas broadcast."

There were a couple radios in camp, well-hidden, that required electricity. Once, a kriege hooked one up and blew out power to the entire camp. Some prisoners made crystal sets by trading cigarettes to guards for wire, lead, and earphones. Batteries, electricity, and radio tubes were not needed for this type of radio. Earl constructed his by dropping a piece of red-hot lead into cold water. A crystal formed on it, and became a hot spot that picked up radio waves. The crystal unit was small, so it was stored between two plastic lids when not in use. The tuning coil was fashioned from a margarine tube. Waxed paper was heated to coat it with wax, then insulated wire was secured to one end, and wrapped in a continuous, neat coil around the outside of the waxed tube's length. The wire was secured, then another coat of wax applied to insulate the coils. When the wax cooled, a nail was used to bare a straight line of metal across the tight coils. A metal slide bar was formed to run back and forth across the bared coils, allowing different stations to be picked up. A length of insulated wire ran from the slide bar and was secured to a small metal plate that could be laid against the crystal, allowing a small bit of exposed wire to touch the hot spot. Earphones were connected to the slide bar with insulated wire. Another wire was hooked to antenna wires hidden in woodwork throughout the barracks.

The safest time to listen was at night. Earl heard all sorts of things. By moving the slider bar across the coils, British Broadcasting, Russian, Polish, French, and German channels were picked up. The pro-axis propaganda of Axis Sally and her cohort, Bruno, was heard early in January, 1944, after American landings at Anzio. Earl heard Tokyo Rose, and learned of the Bitch of Buchanwald who made lampshades of human skin and was especially fond of tattoos.

Weather reports were all alike. Cold, snow, and more on the way, a bitter cold, worse than he'd ever experienced. Making matters worse, the Germans conducted searches for contraband, right after Red Cross parcels were distributed.

Prisoners were ordered outside for spur of the moment roll calls. Officers and guards ransacked, taking cigarettes and food from parcels and hidden stashes, leaving some prisoners with only what they'd hidden on themselves. Searches took time. Men shivered in the yards, in sleet, snow, and excruciating cold.

At one point, during winter, the commandant was positive someone had hidden a radio in a barracks. Guards searched while prisoners stood outside all day for several days in cold, drenching rain, sleet and snow. Prisoners were allowed in only at night. Soon, Earl couldn't feel his hands or feet.

On one occasion, an officer allowed the men to stay inside while he searched the attic crawlspace. A guard entered, carrying a ladder. The officer took it, told him to watch the prisoners, strode further into the barracks where the access hole was, propped the ladder up, climbed it, then entered the attic.

The guard accepted an American cigarette, and was promptly engaged in conversation with some of the men while, midway in the barracks, saws made from cans cut undersides of

179

ladder rungs until about three-quarters through, then disappeared along with their employers.

The officer stuck his head out of the hole, summoned the guard, turned, stepped back onto the ladder and..., then..., with rungs collapsing one after another, went straight to the floor.

He stood for a few moments, holding both sides of the ladder, a too-proud-to-acknowledge-this expression plastered on his face and, then, with a curt smile..., let the pieces fall.

The white-faced guard followed him out of the barracks. Earl watched them go.

"Guys..., I have a feeling we'll be standing out in the yard again when they decide to do another search." He looked at the ladder. "All right...! Firewood!"

May, 1944, German documentation indicated that two-thousand, nine-hundred, seventy-nine American airmen were being held prisoner in Stalag XVII-B. Earl figured at least half of them had spent the winter taking the camp apart, piece by piece, to keep from freezing to death. Doors, benches, fence posts, gate wood, bed slats, parts of walls, ceilings and attics, books, letters from home, ladders, anything burnable that could be done without, went into the stoves.

Spring arrived, with half-frozen mud and rain to stand in during roll calls. Disease ran rampant throughout all of the compounds. Earl became ill, feverish, and was so weak, he went to bed. His throat burned, and he had trouble breathing.

"Can't.... be.... sick. Get up, Benson...." He sat up, then collapsed. Gene carried him to the infirmary.

"What seems to be your problem?" asked the doctor.

"Feel like someone beat the crap outta me, throat's fulla crud..., hurts.... like hell..., can't breathe."

The doctor peered into a throat full of thick pus nodules.

"Diptheria.... I'll have to put you into isolation."

180

Earl stared down at his hands.

No...! God..., this can't be happening.... Isolation... is death... You make it out, fine. If not..., well, too bad, you die....

"Try these pills.... Benson?" The doctor's voice floated into his thoughts, penetrating through fever and pain. Earl blinked, then looked up at him as he repeated, "Sergeant, I want you to take these sulfa pills. It's all I can give you." Earl stared at the doctor's face as he took the pills and a cup of water.

"Oh, man! It's in your eyes, the way you said it..., I'm.... gonna die." He choked down the huge pills. As they made their way past the painful nodules, tears moistened his eyes.

A guard was summoned. Earl was half-carried into a barracks which was encircled by strands of barbed wire. The smell of death encompassed him as he was put to bed.

Days passed..., days that took him in and out of consciousness. Too ill to pray..., a mere shadow of a man..., skin and bones rattling and hacking inside an eighty pound body..., he waited for death. Night after long night, half conscious, he listened to men dying around him.

"God..., if You're going to take me..., take me! But..., please..., don't do this to me.... Please....." He tried to lift his head, but couldn't..., the tears in his eyes were just too heavy.

A week passed. Dead prisoners were carried out each morning, and more, fatally ill, brought in. The doctor came in once in awhile, checked Earl's throat, and gave him sulfa pills and water. The pills became easier to swallow.

Another week went by. Earl forced himself to eat, and exercised his limbs until exhausted and sweaty.

"Ain't.... afraid to die but..., God willing, maybe I can beat this thing." He relaxed, took a deep breath. "You must be trying to teach me something, Lord, or You'da taken my miserable ass outta here a long time ago."

One day, the doctor, peered into his throat.

"Benson, don't you have somewhere else you'd rather be? I don't think you need to be here." Earl stared at him.

"Sonofagun.... You said I wouldn't feel my own death! You mean it? I'm not gonna die?" The doctor almost smiled.

"No..., least ways not today. You can be damn-well sure of one thing, Sergeant. Someone up there...," he pointed at the ceiling, "helped you through this."

Back in barracks 29-B, Earl learned Red Cross parcels weren't coming in as often. Shipments were sporadic and there were fewer parcels to go around when they finally did arrive. The number of prisoners had grown. Everyone suffered.

Earl gathered string, stick, bread crumbs and a parcel box, took them out to the yard, set the box down, tied string to one end of the stick, propped it under a side of the box, spread crumbs around, unrolled the string, kicked dirt over it to conceal it, then crouched, out of sight, by the corner of the barracks.

A small bird flew in, landed next to the box, and pecked at the crumbs. Two more birds alit. Bait disappeared as they edged under the box. The string tightened in Earl's hand.

A little more, and I'll have myself a three-course dinner.

"Hey, Benson! Whatcha doing?" The birds scattered and flew. Earl pressed hard fists against his forehead, and moaned.

"Awh crap, Gene, I almost had 'em!"

His next try met with success. Three birds were trapped, he reached under the crate, slipped one out, snapped its neck, set it aside, then repeated the process. He plucked, gutted, cooked, then ate them, barely a mouthful, but delicious, a welcome, temporary respite from hunger. Afterwards, there was always someone trying to catch birds.

While walking one evening, Earl dealt with a Russian prisoner; a pack of cigarettes for a loaf of bread. He peered through the fence at it....

"Damn small, but right now I'd give him two for it." He threw the pack over the fence with an overhand pitch. It landed at the Russian's feet. Earl grinned, then sobered.

"Oh, no, he's not gonna throw like a girl.... They always throw underhand.... Oh..., crap!" The Russian's sidearm pitch sent the bread sailing though the cool night air. It landed on the American side, near the fence, between it and the warning wire. Earl slapped his forehead.

"I gotta get it!" He waited and watched. The tower guard turned his back. Earl ran like hell, bounded over the warning wire, sprinted toward the loaf..., reached for it....

"Splattt....!" Dumdum bullet splintered a post just to the right of his head. Pieces struck him. He fell, spread-eagled, to the ground, head turned toward the tower. Not moving, one eye open.... just enough, he held his breath and watched the guard. Moments passed as the guard eyed him, then picked up the telephone.

Sharp ears heard, "One American.... dead." Earl sucked in a slow, careful breath.

"Fella..., you made a big mistake when you turned your back the first time, now let's see if.... Yes!" The guard turned. Earl was up, over the wire, and between two barracks. He crouched, caught his breath, then stood. Bread tucked under his arm, he strutted toward his barracks, talking to himself.

"You did it, Benson.... just like a cat with nine lives! Boy, you must've been one in a previous life, 'cause their ain't no other explanation. Yep, even God, Himself, would have to agree about tha...."

Ahead of him, in the dark, someone cleared his throat. Earl stopped, midstride, and made out.... Abie Schultz. The gestapo agent, rocking back and forth on the balls of his feet, blocked his path,

Schultz..., all four feet, ten inches, or so, of him, thin as a rail, hands on hips, elbows pointed almost straight out at him, said, "Ah-ah-ahh, Benson!" Earl glared at the man he'd had so many run-ins with.

"You.... egotistical, thievin' bastard! Taking my cigarettes and stuff while I'm outside freezing my ass off. Well, you're not takin' this! I'll...." Schultz smirked.

"Give me the bread.... You know you are not supposed to be doing this." One hand touched the luger in it's holster. Earl scowled..., then handed the loaf over.

"I'm tellin' you.... now, Schultzie. I've taken nothing but a hard time from you. Don't be around when the war's over, 'cause I'll...." Schultz interrupted.

"Oh..., you are kidding with me, Benson. You are angry with me for just a little while.... You want this bread?" His voice was ice-cold. "You are not going to get a piece of this bread." He turned away.

"Stinkin' bastard...! Think you're King Shit...? Well, plain and simple, Schultzie, you're no better than a Hitler heinie wiper! I'm gonna kill your ass when the war's over..., that's a promise.... Don't be around, Abie, 'cause you'll be kaput..., finished!" Earl swiped a stiff finger across his throat, as the agent faced him again, gun drawn. Schultz's smile was curt.

"Oh, you would not do that, Sergeant."

"Yeah...? Watch me! You took my bread, Abie. For that and all the other rotten things you've done, I'll kill you. Be there when it's over..., then we'll see what I'll do...." Schultz was left standing alone in the darkness.

CHAPTER SIXTEEN

JUST WHICH SIDE OF THE FENCE

The commandant got a new bicycle, and was able to get around in and outside camp without car and driver, until.... someone stole the conveyance and hid it. Orders were issued. Guards would search until bike and thief were found. Gestapo agents and S.S. troupers joined in. Rumors spread as to the whereabouts of the missing bicycle, but no one talked, and it was never found. It had been shoved, with a long stick, into the deepest depths of a forty-holer. Earl half-grinned.

"Hell..., nobody else got a bike, so what'd he expect?"

June 6th, 1944, word around camp was of the Normandy invasion. D-Day information was reported. The news gave Earl an additional supply of will, determination and hope. It was hope prisoners held on to, so desperately, and this news brought a great deal of new hope to their existence.

Summer of 1944 was a welcome friend. Warmth from the sun sank deep into wasted bodies, as prisoners stood outside for roll calls. Earl took his place in line, while a stocky little guard watched. An officer would soon inspect, and once the men were in order, a proud guard, long French rifle slung over his shoulder, goosestepped back and forth in front of them. Each time he passed, men reached behind him, and dropped sand into his rifle barrel, then topped it with a bright daisy, which bobbed up and down, keeping perfect time. The officer stormed over, yelled, grabbed the rifle, turned it over, shook it, shoved it back into the guard's hands, performed a quick inspection, then stormed away.

It wasn't often prisoners laughed. Most days were grim, dismal reminders, with death lurking around every corner. Earl walked at every opportunity, hoping to get fit. One day, as he moved along, he spotted a group of men standing by the fence staring into the Russian compound.

"Hmmm.... what's going on?" He paused. "Guess there's only one way to find out."

He ambled over, and heard, "Get a load of that one over there!" He peered toward where the man pointed and, for a few moments, gawked with the rest of the group. Scantily clad Russian women, some wearing only a towel, lined up to shower.

"Yeah....," he said, taking in the situation, "Guess I'd want a shower, too, if I worked in the fields all day." He turned away. "I'll take an American girl, anyday."

"Benson!" Gene ran up, a grin on his face. "Didja hear what happened?" Earl cocked an eyebrow.

"No..., but by the look on your face, I'll just bet you're about to tell me." Gene's grin widened.

"Someone fried a guard!"

"Whoa! All right, so how'd that happen?"

"Someone hot wired the fence."

"You're kidding."

"No, man! Know how it was raining? He grabs the wire to open the gate and.... zapp! Knocked to the ground! Don't know if it killed him, or not. I didn't hear nothing about that."

"Knocked for a loop, huh? I guess their's more than one way to fry Kraut."

Earl continued his walk, then headed over to work out with the weights.

"Still eighty-two, or three pounds. Not much, but it's solid muscle, and I gotta keep it that way. America's gonna win

186

this war, and I gotta be ready for whatever comes my way. Anyway..., this gives me something to think about besides my empty stomach."

Winter came, with piercing cold winds and sub zero temperatures. Well into the last part of 1944, the prisoners were a desperate bunch, unbelievably emaciated. News came in that a train had brought a huge load of Red Cross parcels up to Krems. Prisoners were excited. Anxious volunteers were taken out to unload them and bring the boxes into camp.

Later, some went out into the compound to watch the procession come in. Earl was in a group watching the returnees.

"Something's wrong. No one's excited over there."

It wasn't long before someone ran over and said, "Oh, man! You ain't never gonna believe this one, guys!" He had their attention. Everyone gathered around, urging him to continue. "Seems propaganda's got the folks back home all screwed up in their heads."

"Yeah, yeah..., so? What the hell did they do this time?"

"Well, fellas..., seems the Germans have been telling America that we're all over here having ourselves a good ole time, playing sports, lounging by swimming pools, and a lot of other bullcrap."

"So?" said Earl. "That figures. What the hell's it got to do with our parcels?"

"Hey! Hang on. I'm getting to that part!" The men stepped back and forth, one foot to the other, and blew warm breath onto their freezing hands.

"Okay..., they get the crates off the train and take a look in some, you know..., 'cause they don't look like what we got before and..., man, that's when it got really crazy." He paused, sucked in a deep breath. "Hell, guys..., we got ourselves ten thousand hockey sticks and a whole mess of pucks, so we can entertain our jolly selves out on the hockey fields this winter!" He looked around the group.

Finally, someone asked, "You mean we didn't get any food boxes?" The once boastful newsbearer shook his head.

"No, that's it, just hockey sticks and pucks." A number of men shook their heads, and walked away. Earl was stunned.

"Hockey fields?" A remaining man smiled grimly.

"Hey, guys..., cheer up.... Least we have firewood for a while, for the coldest nights..., right?"

He was right. It didn't last long, but helped, pucks and sticks burned when temperatures fell to a numbing forty below.

Cigarettes, more valuable than ever, were traded, mostly for articles of clothing. Men wore layers of whatever they could get their hands on, but still shook miserably in their bunks.

Christmas eve, Earl lay in his quarter of the bunk, under the pressed-fiber blanket, listening to his crystal set, earphone cupped in the palm of his hand against his ear, the back of his hand against the thin mattress.

A guard entered to see if everyone was in their bunk. As he walked through, light shone from a squeeze-powered flashlight which whirred noisily when cranked. The beam lit Earl's face. Feigning deep sleep, he snored, copying brother Red's log-sawing. The guard continued down the row. Earl rolled onto his back and stared at the ceiling.

"Figured that'd come in handy sometime, or another."

The guard left and, except for some genuine snoring, things were quiet. Moonlight illuminated the rafters.

Something skampered up the blanket. Earl held his breath as it ran from feet to torso. He peered downward.

Poised on his chest, looking him straight in the face, whiskers twitching, was a tiny mouse.

"Merry Christmas, ya little cheese thief," whispered Earl.

"Now git outta here, or I'll eat you." With a quick flip of the blanket, the visitor was gone. Earl, rolled to one side, felt and heard his stomach growling.

"Damn this hunger!" He drew his knees to his chest.

"When's this Godforsaken war gonna be over?" The moon slipped behind a cloud. In darkness, he thought of wonderful Christmas mornings his family had spent together, pictured faces, gleaming with anticipation, as they sat around the big, formal dining table. He envisioned the huge holiday dinner, each delicious dish passed from one hand to another. A tear rolled down toward the crystal set. He wiped it away.

"Benson..., you're not doing this. Won't do a damn bit of good. Concentrate on the broadcast." The announcer was talking about a new song.

"Now, here's something for all the guys over there who are fighting for freedom. Hope you'll all be home... real soon."

For the first time, since the beginning of his long journey into hell, Earl allowed himself to let go without shame filling each tear that rolled down his cheeks. There was no way he could have stopped himself..., as a new, young singer, Bing Crosby, crooned into his ear....

"I'll be home for Christmas..., You can count on me...."

Next day, Christmas, thirty below, most of the camp's forty-five hundred American airmen were rousted out into the snow for roll call. Others were too ill to move from their bunks. Pneumonia and chilblains were common. The prisoners were a cold, hungry bunch. Lice and fleas had taken a toll on their bodies, infecting them with scabies and other diseases.

Barely enough Red Cross parcels were saved up for the day. Boxes were distributed throughout all the barracks. Five hollow-eyed men were assigned to each box, and instructed to divide the contents equally among themselves. After all..., this was Christmas and this was their Christmas present. Earl was reminded of all the presents he'd shared with his brothers.

"I just wish this one was several times bigger, so there'd be more to go around." He shrugged. "Then again, I guess we should be thankful for what we got. Ain't much, but least it's something from home and it'll get us through a few more days."

"Water's on!" Cold water ran for a couple of hours in the shower rooms. Spigots were opened, tubs filled, then covered to keep dirt and debris out. This water, to be used later, was strictly for drinking and cooking. Barracks 29-B had gone without heat many nights in order to accumulate firewood for today. Buckets of water boiled on the stove for coffee and tea. Earl hunted up a piece of soap, warmed a wet rag against the side of the stove, then washed some of the grime off of himself.

"Oh, man this feels good." He rinsed the rag, wiped the soap off, then stood near the stove until warm and dry.

The Germans distributed the usual wormy swill, and played Christmas music over recently installed loudspeakers. Earl reasoned that the new sound system was a better way for them to announce roll calls and deliver reprimands.

"This way they don't trounce through mud and snow, from building to building, exposing themselves to disease and vermin. Guess it keeps the bastards from repeating threats and pointless information on bitter cold days like today."

Men sang carols, and morale picked up. Earl ate some of the food from his share of the Red Cross parcel, and kept the rest in his pockets. He stared at the stove.

"If I could just blink..., find myself at home..., but..., I'm here..., thankful just to be alive. So many have died..., and I came too damn close, myself." He stared at the ceiling.

"Save us, Lord," he whispered. "Make more food

available, keep us warm, and see us safely home. I pray this is our last holiday here, and that..., is all I've got to say, so.... Amen." The morning passed.

Later, he was surprised when Bill Hovekamp entered and walked over to him.

"Hey, Benson," he said with quiet excitement. "We got ourselves a rabbit, and want you to come have dinner with us." Earl grinned, and followed Hovekamp.

"Wow, the Lord sure works in mysterious ways!"

They entered barracks 35-A, then stood near the stove, surrounded by men shouting greetings.

"Hey, it's the rascal bellygunner!" and, "Hi, Benson! Merry Christmas, you little turd! You're just in time." The bucket with boiling broth and fully-cooked rabbit was removed from the stove by the cook after he'd wrapped both hands in rags. He set the pot down onto a bench. Earl caught a whiff of the good-smelling meat. The pot tender used a can-derived, fork-like utensil and knife to slice a bite from the carcass.

"Rascal..., since you're the guest of honor here, the first piece goes to you." Earl thanked his host, then gingerly took the meat, which had cooled off in the cold air, between thumb and forefinger. He blew eagerly on it, popped it into his mouth, closed his eyes, then savored the taste as he chewed the tender morsel. The men quieted. Still chewing, he opened his eyes..., found them staring, some wincing, others looking hopeful. He stopped chewing.

"Okay..., what's going on, fellas? You know something I don't?" He chewed again, then stopped....

"This ain't rabbit..., is it?" Laughter filled his ears, but dwindled as Hovekamp spoke.

"Remember the alleycat we had runnin' around camp?" Earl looked hard at Bill, then rolled his eyes toward the ceiling.

"So..., I'm your guinea pig, huh? Thanks, Bill! Thanks a lot, guys!" The cook slapped Earl's shoulder.

"Well..., Rascal, how is it? Did we do it right..., I mean, by boiling it? We figured it would go a lot further that way." Earl looked around the group.

"You know, fellas..., I should say it's the worst piece of crap I ever put into my mouth, but..., honest, guys..., I can't tell the difference 'tween this and rabbit. Tastes like the real McCoy." Cheers and whistles filled the air. Everyone in 35-A had a share of the welcome Christmas meal.

Hovekamp brushed his dark hair back with one hand, and chewed thoughtfully on his small mouthful of the special delicacy. He grinned at Earl.

"Had to have a man who knew wild meat from garbage. Figured, since you'd hunted as a kid and had a damn good sense of humor, that you were the one. 'Sides, I figured you'd appreciate the nourishment and company."

"Well, Bill..., I guess if you cook the hell out of a cat, or dog, there ain't much to worry about..., and I do appreciate it.... Thanks." Bill slapped his back.

"Merry Christmas, Benson!"

Too close to choking up, Earl said, "Merry Christmas, Hovekamp..., and a Happy New Year, too."

That evening, like so many evenings before, Earl sat listening to the newsman. The Goat, as he was called, visited each barracks, at night, giving latest information on the war.

"Now hear this," he said in a sharp voice, so accurate in use of diction, it left nothing to question. "Quiet, everyone!" Anxious men absorbed each word as he read his report.

The Goat described, in detail, the Battle of the Bulge, and the Red Ball express that carried supplies to the front lines. Reports were composed from several sources. Aides spoke and understood German, French, Russian, and Polish. Assistants listened to reports on radios and crystal sets. The Goat told where General Patton's troups were, what progress was made in various battlefields, and assured prisoners that the Americans were advancing and the end of the conflict was near. Men took this information to heart, and used every opportunity to keep the Germans stirred up. Everyone knew the opposition had lost, but Earl doubted the Germans would ever concede the fact.

One day, a general and his officers entered barracks 29-B and had a look at the map. They stood, hands clasped behind backs, and studied it. A few men, including Earl and Gene, positioned themselves nearby. They watched and listened as the stiff jawed general tapped the board with a finger.

"Nicht richtig! Es ist nicht~zu lugen." Earl frowned.

"What's he mean it's not right? He has the gall to stand there and call us liars?" Like a bantam rooster, he stepped up, and tapped the board. Gene's mouth fell open..., as did others.

"Ist richte! Sieh her!" Earl tapped a line. The general and his officers stared at him. "Patton here! Boom! Ist richte! Patton boommm!" Smile cold, the general cocked an eyebrow.

"Du bist wohl nicht ganz~." Turning sharp on his heels, he clicked out of the barracks, followed by the officers.

"What'd he say?" asked Earl.

"Du bist wohl nicht ganz~, Benson," said a barracksmate.

"Yeah," said Gene as he began to goosestep across the floor. "In plain English, the general just said you must be out of your mind!" The goosestepper was joined by a few more men.

"Ein gross rascal bellygunner bist wohl nicht ganz~!"

"You are crazy, man!" Gene stopped short in front of Earl, then saluted.

"Sergeant Benson," he clipped, "You sure as hell have a lot of nerve, telling Herr general just which side of the fence the old bear took a crap on!" Earl grinned a chin jutting grin.

"Well, fellas..., I calls 'em like I sees 'em. If they don't like it, well..., that's just tough!"

Bulletin boards showcased artwork. The camp had a cartoonist who'd been an animator for Walt Disney. He drew caricatures of the Seven Dwarfs flying American fighter planes and bombers on their way to rescue beautiful Snow White. Earl enjoyed seeing those and others that made it onto the boards.

February 3, 1945, German records stated there were four thousand, two hundred and forty-two American Airmen held prisoner in Stalag XVII-B.

Many of these happy-go-lucky, hockey playing fellows were frolicking beneath barracks with sand buckets and shovels, doing a whole lot of tunnel digging to see if they could escape from the sandbox without getting caught. In reality, it was serious business, something positive to do, a never-stop-trying effort. Everyone knew freedom was just around the corner, but this digging activity had become compulsive, something to keep minds and bodies occupied, and keep hope alive day after day. Tremendous amounts of dirt had to be hidden. Eventually, shower drains clogged, so men emptied dirt from holes in their pockets as they walked around the compound.

The men in barracks 29-B started a tunnel beneath the huge iron washtub in the shower room. Water from the tub was transferred into buckets so it could be moved while the tunnel was worked on. It was near impossible to hide the dirt, and too many men in other barracks were being caught. Patton's troups were advancing quickly across Germany toward Austria, so the tunnel was filled in under 29-B.

A saboteur, broke in, to get food, rest, and information from prisoners. Guards searched, positive he was in camp, but the man hid a couple nights. The search escalated, and he hid in a toilet, up to his neck in waste, until it was called off.

Early April, the American Air Force bombed Krems. Guards, some who'd lost family, returned to camp the next day, and fired their guns at prisoners. Later that day, American P-38s flew over, so low, Earl, along with others, saw pilots give a definite thumbs up. Prisoners cheered and waved.

Orders came in to the commandant from Hitler, directing him to have all of the prisoners killed. The commandant issued orders. Prisoners were to ready themselves to evacuate camp.

Stalag 17-B   1945

April 10th, of 1945, the prisoners, under close guard, were force-marched out of Stalag XVII-B. The cleaned up saboteur now hid among the Americans.

Most of the Russian prisoners had been ground troups. When the camp was evacuated, thirty-five to forty thousand Russians walked out.

Every prisoner coming out of Stalag XVII-B was well aware he had a long, perilous trek ahead of himself. American and British troups were approaching from the west. Russian troups were coming in from the east. The Germans were caught in the middle; the prisoners at their mercy.

As the men walked, day after day, in bitter cold sleet and snow, ears, noses, feet and hands froze. They got one bowl of soup and a slice of bread per day, but sometimes didn't get that.

Several days passed. Sticks were found, helping men walk, until the wood was added to night fires. Frozen hands and feet thawed each evening and refroze each day.

Almost another week passed. Walking, daylight to dusk, the group headed toward Braunau and the border of Bavaria by the Inn river, two hundred and eighty-seven miles from Krems. They were strafed with friendly fire by American, English, and Russian fighters. The Red Cross had indicated that prisoners were to wave their hats so everyone would know they were Americans. Everything happened so fast, that some flyers didn't get the word, and.... there were many casualties.

Earl's friend, Gene, walked beside him. Halfway into the treacherous journey, at Linz, Austria, they were about to cross the Enns river bridge. As they approached, shells dropped by allied forces exploded around them. There was no turning back. Men screamed. Everyone ran, trying to get across the span.

Earl got to the bridge as a bomb exploded, knocking him flat on his face. Blood curdling screams came from behind him. He raised and turned to look for Gene, who'd just been there..., right on his heels, but his friend was nowhere to be seen. Bloodied men rushed by, almost stepping on him. Some carried or dragged injured. Earl struggled to his feet.

"Gotta find him!" Panicked men pushed by; more rushed at him, blocking his view. He ducked through them and..., saw Gene..., pinned..., like a rag doll on a clothesline, his limp, lifeless body hung on the side of a concrete building..., smashed against the wall by the same concussion that had knocked Earl down. Blood ran from ears, nose, and mouth. Eyes..., that moments before.... had been filled with hope and determination, now stared..., wide open in death.

"Noooooo...!" Earl's scream blended itself into thousands of others. He stumbled as more men ran by. He fought to take a step toward Gene, but was knocked back when another shell exploded. Terrified, ears ringing, he turned and ran onto the blood slickened bridge. Men opened mouths, emitting screams and shouts, all around him, but it sounded faint and distorted, as if he were underwater. He was swept along, as desperation and fear pushed and shoved men across the bridge. He slipped and went down on one knee.

"Gotta stay on my feet!" Grabbing a man's pantleg as he stumbled by, Earl regained footing and made it to the end of the bridge. Glancing back, he saw the span.... littered with bodies.

Guards shouted orders; a few fired warning shots into the air. Lives were at stake; order was quickly regained among the prisoners as they hurried up the road.

Almost three weeks passed. Weeks filled with agonizing pain, discomfort, hunger, fear..., suffering. In no man's land, starving, half-frozen skeletons put one foot in front of the other.

Many men..., too many..., have been killed each day. Others fall, and die on the road, too sick to endure another moment of torture. The Russian front is coming up the Danube Valley, and the prisoners from Stalag XVII-B are being force-marched right out in front of them. The prisoners have to move fast in order to avoid being caught in the middle of a heated battle between Russian and German forces, both of whom are pressed toward them by Patton's troups. Earl peers ahead and sees a large group of prisoners coming at them.

The distance between them closes, then someone ahead of him says, "Gawd..., they're Jews!" Earl shadows his eyes.

"They're going the wrong way." The group moves closer. He stumbles..., mouth falls open.

"My..., God...! I thought we were in bad shape..., that no one could be worse off than us..., but..., all of them are! They're walking dead men!" Fingers touch the crumbs in his pocket..., but the men from XVII-B have been instructed not to give the desperate Jewish prisoners any food, because 'they'll kill each other over the tiniest scrap.'

Fists ball up in helpless frustration. A knot rises in his throat... as he spots two Jewish men dragging a third between themselves. The knees of their ragged, dirty pants.... are torn and soaked with blood. He swallows hard....

"Death...." The trio of skeletons collapse onto their knees into a small drift along the roadway.... The pure white snow.... turns crimson. These men.... cannot raise their heads. If they could, they would see sheer terror in Earl's eyes as a German officer strides over and..., without a word, raises his weapon.

One..., two..., three... shattering reports crash against Earl's eardrums as each man is shot..., point blank, in the head.

Filled with horror, he sees them fall face-first into the snow, sees.... their eyes glaze over..., sees them die...., feels himself filling with grief and rage.

He moves toward the officer.

Grabbed from behind, stopped short, Earl is spun around, and a friend's eyes meet his with a cold, hard look that leaves no doubt. Casey has not spoken, nor does he need to.

The look says, "This rage must be controlled.... Today is not the day for you to die. Put this behind you, and.... go on."

Casey stumbles along beside him.

Days before, Earl had watched, angered, when Casey was struck by a guard after refusing to put out a fire. The guard was massive. His huge skull and crossbones ring had split Casey's lip wide open when he'd slammed his fist into it. Earl had talked Casey out of going after the guard..., had stopped him from killing his aggressor.

Now, Earl glances at his friend and notices the lower lip is still swollen and looks infected. He clings to Casey's ragged shirttail, and is half-pulled along.

He closes his eyes. Horrifying replays form on the backs of their lids.

Skeletons fall..., gunshots ring out.... once..., twice..., three times..., he sees Gene's body..., smashed..., lifeless..., against the wall..., hears Dave screaming..., "Bensonnn.....!"

That night, he dreams.... He is walking.... An endless road stretches ahead, a road strewn.... with broken violins. He is running, picking up pieces, crying..., holding them tight to his chest. He hears himself begging other prisoners....

"Oh, God...! Please...! Doesn't anyone have any glue?" The pieces turn into body parts, dripping with blood. Horrified, he drops them..., then stares ahead.... at an endless road.... filled with dead men and body parts, as far as he can see.

The next day, Earl put his slice of bread in a pocket, after breaking it into small pieces, a reminder to himself to nibble, and not be tempted to eat all of it at once. He drank his soup, and watched Casey pour part of his own ration into a jar, screw the lid on tight, then drop it into a pocket. He wished he had a jar, or better yet, a canteen like some men had.

That night, after setting up camp in a field, his group sat around a fire, thawing hands and feet. One man laid his canteen near the flames to warm the water inside. Exhausted, the prisoner propped a foot atop it. The heated canteen would help keep him warm later, as he slept. Tired as hell, cold, hungry..., that's what they all were as they sat, trying to get warm, their feet nearly in the flames.

"Ka-blamm!" Men ducked and jumped.

"Oh, my Gawd! Oh, my Gawd! My foot! Oh, Gawwwd!" From across the fire, someone shouted.

"What the hell happened?" As men gathered, it became clear. The man hadn't loosened the cap on the canteen. Steam built up pressure as water boiled inside the metal container. The canteen exploded and blew half its owner's boot and foot off. The man rocked back and forth in agony. Someone tied a rag around his ankle. A sickening, salty taste filled Earl's mouth.

"Oh, God, I'm gonna be sick..., which is ridiculous. I've seen a hell of a lot worse than this." He clamped his hand over his mouth. "Oh, man..., I've gotta get away from here!" He walked to another group, stood near their fire, and collected himself. When he returned to his group, the man's foot was wrapped in rags. The useless boot, minus laces, lay nearby in the bloodied snow, the laces used to secure rags around what was left of the owner's foot.

May 4th, they moved through Braunau. Twenty-four bone chilling days since walking out of Stalag XVII-B.

On the twenty-fifth day, they walked through a barbed wire gate into some woods on the east bank of the Inn river. The prisoners were told that this was their new home. Ominous strands of double barbed wire fencing surrounded the huge area, and guards were posted all along the outer perimeter.

When they'd begun the forced march, there were approximately forty-five hundred American Airforce prisoners in the group. Now there were about four thousand. Some five hundred Americans had perished along the way.

The prisoners were instructed to build their own houses. Men built fires, then lean-tos, in an effort to ease the numbing effects of the bitter cold. Many, including Earl, feared that if the Germans panicked, prisoners would be machine gunned to death. Some tried to dig holes in the frozen ground to scramble into should gunfire erupt. This activity was nearly impossible, with no shovels or tools and energy levels so low. Still, they did all they could to improve their lot.

Snow fell. Temperatures plummeted. Men continued to dig, and gather firewood in order to have a night's worth of fuel. Across the river, a German S.S. division was all that stood between them and Patton's troups. One hell of a battle was taking place over there. The prisoners heard shells exploding only a couple of miles away. They sang well-known American songs to establish their presence to any ground troups that might cross the river, and hoped none of the bombs would miss their target and fall into camp. A bucket brigade was escorted back and forth from camp to the river. When men returned with water and information, the men in camp grew more excited. Finally, a prisoner came back with news.

"Patton's troups are right across the river! One of our guys sneaked off, and swam it to let them know we're here."

That evening, an American Army captain crossed the river in a pontoon. As his group strode up to the German commandant, Earl spotted the forty-five in the captain's holster. A sergeant with a Thompson submachine gun accompanied him.

"We are coming across the river tomorrow," said the captain to the commandant. "If you are smart, you will comply with the laws set forth by the Geneva Convention. I'm warning you right now. For every American that you shoot, we will shoot two of your men."

The next morning, a lieutenant arrived with troups. The Germans began handing their guns over.

CHAPTER SEVENTEEN

I KEEP MY PROMISES

"Hallelujah! Oh..., God..., it's over!" Most who heard this absurd shouting, didn't react.

"We're free!" yelled another man, racing wildly through camp. "It's for real, guys! We're gettin' outta here.... going home!" Men ran about, shouted, and pounded one another's backs. Some, refusing to believe, continued to tend fires, reinforce lean-tos, and dig. Many were too sick to do anything.

Some S.S. Troupers, unwilling to turn themselves in, had hidden in the woods. The ex-prisoners were instructed with, "Go out, find as many Germans as possible, and bring their Kraut asses back here. Earl focused on doing what he knew he had to do. Ammunition bandoleers crisscrossed his chest. He tucked a German luger into his belt.

"Now the Germans are behind the barbed wire." Machine pistol in hand, he helped round up some of the enemy, and remove their weapons.

He searched the outer perimeter of the enclosure, away from the river, toward the back of the camp.

"Okay, Benson..., toe-heel, keep low..., like Howard showed you way back when...." A sound... twigs snapping.... He crouched..., peered through the brush.... "Something over there...., man hunkered down by that tree.... He raised his pistol. German uniform...., he's turning....,

"Schultz!" Heart beat crashed against eardrums.

"Abieeee...!" Twenty-five months..., spent watching the

slow, gruesome deaths of huge numbers of men, and seeing countless others die in an instant, had boiled to a head. Twenty-five months..., in which he'd felt and witnessed more misery and suffering than in his entire life.

Schultz looked right at him, then ducked and ran.

"I keep my promises, Abie! It's payback time!" The woods were sprayed with machine gun fire, the noise deafening, as twenty-five rounds pelted the area. Here, in this time and place, death meant nothing. This.... was no man's land.

"Die, you son of a bitch...!" He stared into the woods.

"Didn't miss. Unless the bastard's hugging the ground behind a tree, he's dead. If not, I know damn well I put the fear of God in him." Promise kept, he turned and walked toward the front of the camp.

Casey clapped a hand onto Earl's shoulder.

"Hey, Rascal, you look like that Mexican revolutionary leader guy, you know, Pancho Villa." He tried to smile as Earl faced him. Seeing Casey's lip, Earl grimaced.

"It's worse than yesterday, Case..., you've got to see a medic." Casey shook his head.

"Unh uh, Got a better idea. Let's find the son-of-a-bitch that cracked me in the mouth." Earl nodded.

"Hell, yeah, let's go find the bastard." They went to the front of the camp where three or four hundred German prisoners were lined up, guarded by American Army troups.

Earl followed as Casey peered into enemy faces until he spotted the big German. The ex-guard recognized him, and averted his eyes. Casey spoke German.

"You're the bastard who mashed me in the mouth."

"Nein, comrade." The big man's face forced calmness. Casey strode over to an American Army sergeant.

"Let me borrow your gun." The sergeant's eyes

narrowed.

"Why?"

"Because..., I don't want to use a German gun. I want to use an American gun." The sergeant shrugged, then handed over his gun. Casey tucked it into his waist band, then returned to where Earl stood, gun aimed at the ex-guard. He pointed.

"Rascal, grab that shovel." Earl retrieved it. The sergeant looked curious, but turned his attention to other things. Earl heard Casey order the German into the woods. He followed, along a path that led toward the rear of the camp, on the opposite side from where he'd seen Schultz. They left the path, entered the woods, and stopped. Earl handed the shovel over. Casey thrust it into the German's big hands.

"Dig. The German pleaded. Casey aimed the gun.

"Dig until I tell you to stop." The shovel was forced into the ground until a hole had been dug.

"Stop," said Casey. Ranting in German, he drew a two-foot by six-foot oblong line around the hole with the toe of his shoe. Earl stood back, watching the surrounding woods for movement. Casey's voice was commanding, cold.

"Deeper." Enlarging the hole, the German dug a foot more into the hard ground, grunting with each shovel thrust.

"Lay down!" Trembling, pleading, he lay face down.

"Turn over!" The man turned, and stared up into the cold, dismal, winter-gray sky. Casey knelt and held the gun to his forehead. Bitter cold as it was, Earl saw beads of sweat glistening on the German's brow. Casey grinned down at him.

"You're gonna die...." He pulled the trigger.... Earl felt sick, gut-wrenching tugs in the pit of his stomach, as the gun clicked. The German jumped.

There was no report....

"Not deep enough," said Casey. "Get up. Dig some

more." Earl watched Casey replace the clip he'd removed.

"Why in hell are you playing games? C'mon, Case, Pete's sake, get it done! Someone'll walk up on us. Ca...,"

"Enough...!" The forty-five thundered. The German was dead, a hole between wide-open, blue eyes. Earl drew a sharp breath and turned away. Casey yanked the skull and crossbones ring from the dead man's finger, then flung it into the woods.

"Ain't never gonna happen to anyone else!"

A civilian, on a bicycle, left the pathway, stopped next to them, then stepped off of the bike. Wide eyes took in the scene.

"What is going on? What has happened here?" Casey picked up the shovel and threw it at him.

"If you do not want to join him, you had best cover him up. Do it quick, or you will be dead in the hole with him." Eyes wide, the civilian shoveled dirt and snow into the hole.

"If...," said Casey, "ya know what's good for you, you'll get back on your bike and leave. You didn't see anything." The civilian dropped the shovel and scrambled onto his bicycle.

"I did not see anything!" The man sped away, then disappeared into the distance. Casey picked up the shovel and, without a word or backward glance, headed toward the front of the camp. Earl shook his head, and followed.

The Army sergeant met them.

"Where's my gun?" Casey returned the forty-five.

"By the way," said the sergeant, "I didn't see anything either." He turned and walked away. Casey headed up the roadway, leaving Earl without a word. Earl followed for a short distance, then gave up.

"Probably wants to be alone. Go figure."

A jeep pulled alongside. An Army officer grinned at him.

"Lo, there! I'm looking for someone to ride with us and man the machine gun." He nodded toward the back of the jeep.

Earl eyed the big gun mounted there.

"It's worth a field commission to you," said the officer as Earl stepped along beside the jeep.

Nose wrinkled, brow furrowed, Earl said, "Huh! What happened to the guy you had? Thanks, but no thanks, sir." He pointed a finger, and said, "You're going that way...." Sticking his thumb out and waggling it to point in the opposite direction, he grinned, then said, "and I'm going this way!" The officer roared with laughter.

"Are you absolutely sure?"

"Damn right I am, sir.... I'm going home!" The officer grinned, and waved as the jeep moved up the road. Earl turned. Casey had disappeared. He sighed.

"Story of my life."

A colonel arrived and informed the ex-prisoners, "It's going to be three days, or so, before Army transports arrive. Soon as they do, we'll get you out of here and on your way home. We have to go on ahead, so you take care of yourselves. You've got the guns and ammunition to do it. Do anything you want. Take anything you want. Sleep anywhere you want. Do not kill unless they try to kill you, and do not rape the women."

Earl and a couple of friends went into town, and were quicky invited to stay in a civilian's home. Their host, a friendly sort, limped about on a peg leg, begging the Americans to stay. As Earl shook the man's hand, he saw fear in his eyes.

"If the Russians come into his house, there's a damn-good chance they'll murder him, rape his wife and daughter, then kill them, too." The trio decided to grant the man's wish.

The family was thrilled to have the airmen there. Mugs were filled from a barrel of hard cider from the cellar, refills.... unlimited. The wife prepared wonderful meals, not much, but plenty for shrunken stomachs. Earl and his friends were given a featherbed to sleep in.

That night, as he lay in luxurious comfort in the soft bed covered with soft, hand-woven blankets, in cozy warmth, Earl let out a long sigh.

"My dear God..., I swear I've died and gone to heaven. Pinch me, guys. I've got to be dreaming!" They pinched him.

The next morning, their hostess smiled a sad smile when they entered her warm kitchen.

"I would like to make apple strudel for you, but I do not have everything it takes." Earl grinned at her.

"Well, we'll just have to see what we can do about that."

After breakfast, the threesome headed to the village square. They raided the bakery, taking apples, flour, sugar, baking powder, eggs, butter, and all of the things they figured a family could use, packing it into huge cooking pots.

As they carried the supplies up the street, they noticed a good deal of frenzied activity coming from the bank. Ex-prisoners had strode in, waving guns. Earl heard yelling.

"This is a stick up! Give us all the dough!" Earl hooted.

"Wait a minute..., I thought we had all the dough!" Moments later, money, stacks of it, was thrown into the street. Villagers scrambled about, gathering, shrieking and shouting joyously. Ex-prisoners stuffed money into their pockets. Earl reached down, picked up a huge wad of paper money, looked at it for a moment, then stuffed it into his pocket.

When they arrived at the cottage, he gave it to their startled host, who shook Earl's hand until the airman thought it would fall off. Earl grinned, then headed for the kitchen.

"Money can't buy everything. I've got strudel on my mind!" Eyes huge, their hostess ushered them into her kitchen, laughing and crying, as the supplies were set on the table.

"Oh..., you dear men! Oh, you make me so happy!" She patted her face dry with the corner of her apron, then shooed them from the kitchen.

From the front porch, they heard her humming and singing. Earl's mouth watered. He looked over at his friends.

"Still can't believe we're free, guys. I hear a bunch have died.... Much as we'll be tempted, we have to be careful about eating. Our systems won't handle it if we over do it. Best keep in mind to eat small amounts..., and realize that food's available anytime we want it." His friends nodded.

Earl wore his guns, even at night, and eyed everyone who came anywhere near the house. Soon it was time to leave. Their hosts were sad for themselves, but thrilled for them. Everyone hugged. With tear-filled eyes, their hostess kissed each airman on both cheeks. The family waved, and the woman and daughter blew kisses until the men were out of sight.

Ex-prisoners gathered, and were transported by truck to an airfield where they waited to be flown out. There were many groups ahead of Earl's. He approached the pilot of a C-47 transport, and said, "Put me on with this next load..., and I'll give you my six-shooter." The pilot's smile was apologetic.

"Sorry, sergeant. Sure wish I could bargain with you, but we have to take everyone in order."

When Earl's group was ready to fly, he eagerly boarded.

They flew to Camp Lucky Strike in France, were sprayed with DDT, given military haircuts, then directed to the showers.

Earl tied his shoe laces with tight, neat bows, then smiled.

"Haircut, hot water, soap, shampoo, towel, shaving gear, new clean clothes from the skin out, jacket, socks, shoes.... Now I know I've died and gone to heaven! Everything's two sizes too big, but I haven't looked this good since Lord knows when."

Moral was back. Several men were short sheeted. Earl

slid into bed, then yawned.

"Wish I had the energy it took. Feels so good to climb between clean, white sheets."

In the following days, he found it pure delight to look at three squares a day and wonder where the devil he was going to put all the food. Portions were not big, but for him, it was too much. His pockets filled with crackers, fruit and bread. There was always food or drink in his hand. He was a constant nibbler, and now weighed.... about eighty-six pounds.

May 5th, 1945, exactly twenty-five months from the day he'd been shot down, Earl was required to sign a certificate. It stated, essentially, that he would not disclose any military information to unauthorized persons, now or later as a civilian. He was officially a repatriated American.

Back home, his mother was notified by telegram that he'd been returned to American military control on May 3rd, 1945.

Earl's group boarded a merchant marine ship at LeHavre, France. The vessel was with the last convoy crossing to the United States. Her captain zigzagged her all the way to America in order to avoid U-boats full of Germans who were unaware that the war was over.

The ship's merchant marine crewmen were drinking and having a good time. Three days out of port they held a fire drill. Everyone was ordered up on deck. When Earl returned to quarters, his barracks bag was missing. He searched the area.

"Gone..., all of it! Flying jacket, guns, coins, swastikas, armbands, German officer helmets, the tunics with the shoulder epaulets... Damn...! Won't do any good to ask about it, either..., hell, I'll never find any of it on this barge!" He stormed out of his quarters, and headed up on deck to smoke a cigarette.

"Sons a bitches! That was my stuff! I hope the thievin' rat shoots himself, or falls overboard!"

As he stood at the rail on deck, anger eased off into the setting sun.

"Guess it's better this way. That stuff would never do nothing but remind me of a bad time."

Friends had gone their own ways. He shrugged it off.

"Guess I didn't know 'em as well as I thought. Gene and Dave were true friends... ones I could really count on are dead." He took a piece of gum from his shirt pocket, unwrapped it, then slid it into his mouth. Hattie popped into his head.

"Huh...! I wonder if she's still at the diner? Shoot, she probably won't remember me..., but, she said I reminded her of her son, and told me to come see her when I get back...." He smiled to himself, and tapped the railing.

"Well, I'm back, and I know just what I'm gonna do. I'm gonna march right into that diner and order steak, fries..., and the biggest vanilla shake that was ever made!"

Documents of surrender were signed. The war in Europe was over. President Roosevelt designated May 8, 1945 Victory in Europe Day.

Earl listened to music from the ship's speakers. There were many new songs, all upbeat and exciting. Glenn Miller and his orchestra played "In The Mood," and "Elmer's Tune." He heard "Chattanooga Choo-Choo," and "Fools Rush In," as he wandered about.

"Going home.... don't need any so-called friends now and, apparently..., they don't need me. Hard-faced, he stopped at the rail and lit a cigarette."

"Hey, Sarge!" The strong voice came from behind.

"Think you could fix us up with a smoke?" Earl frowned, reached for the pack in his pocket, turned..., and found himself facing five men.... in baskets.... No arms.... No legs.

211

There was no hesitation. Like a magnet to cold, hard steel, he was drawn to them, then hit it off when he said the first thing that popped into his head.

"Now..., how in hell.... did you guys manage to get yourselves into this predicament?" They started talking at once.

Time passed quickly as they told their stories, joked, and argued points.

They threatened Earl with, "Watch it, buster or I'll come over there and box your ears off!" Earl laughed.

"Guess you would be hard-pressed if someone actually boxed them off." The reply was quick.

"Naww! What's one more missing body part to a bunch a tough birds like us? Hell, we'd never miss the damn things!"

Earl listened, enjoyed their gutsy self-contradictions, and added to the conversation. He lit cigarettes and held them to appreciative lips. It occured to him to ask them a hard question.

"Was it worth it, guys..., I mean, I know..., I'd do it all again..., and soon's I get fit, I'm gonna go fight the Japs....

"Hell, yes...! they chorused. The man nearest spoke, his voice fervent.

"If this...." he jutted his chin downward, "means my kids and grandkids will never have to go through what I did.... to preserve, defend, and guarantee their freedom...., then you're damn right I'd do it again!" Earl patted his shoulder.

The ship approached New York Harbor.

Earl left the men, walked over to the railing, then tapped it with appreciative fingertips as he heard the Andrews Sisters, accompanied by Vic Schoen and his orchestra, singing Rum and Coca-Cola.

The men had a bird's-eye view, as Lady Liberty stood proud before them, arm bearing the torch of freedom raised high to touch the sky.

Sunshine warmed Earl's drawn, hardened face.... Soon he'd be walking down the streets of Unionville. His thin hands gripped the railing. Glancing back at the five quadriplegics, he saw their eyes.... full of tears....

Gripping the railing tighter, he turned away..., and felt those tears.... took them deep into a heart..., which overfilled..., and spilled them..., into his own eyes.

He drew a ragged breath..., blinked. Burning, hot tears cascaded down his cheeks, and..., that.... was okay....

The Rascal bellygunner was home.

AFTERWORD

Earl Benson didn't know until forty-seven years later that of the original twenty planes that went on the April 5, 1943 mission to bomb the Erla Works, four were shot down. Two returned early. Seventeen were over the target, but one was unable to drop its bombs and jettisoned later. Fourteen B-17s landed safely back in England at 4:58 PM.

An April '86 issue of "306TH ECHOES" contained a four-page coverage of "The Mission To Erla," wherein are statements such as, "Probably most determined attack and hottest fight seen by our forces in this theatre," and "Our crews feel enemy is desperate and enemy proves his desperation by variety and intensity of his efforts to stop accurate bombing of American forces. Yellow-nose FWs closed, time after time, in head-on attacks, coming back, immediately, to attack formation by continuous attack by numbers of enemy aircraft attacking from every angle. There seems to be no question that FW is being used to drop bombs on formation. Many crews report seeing both bombs and explosions. One bombardier says bombs are carried externally, between folded wheels. Another officer states he has seen bomb clearly enough to say it has fins."

The above quotes came from the intelligence teletype report to the Commanding General, First Bomb Wing.

Until March, 1990, Earl couldn't remember names of men he'd trained with or been shot down with. He still can't recall names of many, having blocked them out. In his story, fictional names have been given to Hattie, Mack, Sonny, Dave, Gene, and Casey. Hope is that someone reading the account will recognize a portrayal and provide identity.

In 1990, I discovered "First Over Germany - A History Of The 306 Bombardment Group" by Russell A. Strong, and showed it to Earl.

"Weren't you with the 306th?" He nodded.

"What day were you shot down?"

"April 5th, 1943." It was in chronological order.

Turning to Chapter 7, page 82, I read, "Losses Mount Rapidly, April 1943." Halfway down, I read, "Shot down over the Erla Works was Lt. Kelly Ross' 367th plane. Becoming prisoners with Ross were Lts. George Lewis and Sidney Miller, and Sgts. Earl Benson, William Hovekamp, Clyde Smith and Douglas Bowles. T/Sgt. Arnold E. Hyman and S/Sgt. Arthur Byrd, tail gunner and waist gunner, did not survive."

A beginning for, "Out Of The Turret And Into Hell." I wrote letters and got answers. Now Earl had some names to put with faces while I probed, taped his talks with friends about World War II, and interviewed him.

March, 1993 we got a letter from Belgium historian, Jean Dillen, a teenager when the Erla Werks was bombed. Jean let us to know he was writing a book called "Erlawerk VII", and needed Earl's story. I sent "The Fifth Mission." We received an autographed copy of his book, written in Deutch-Flemish with an exerpt in English pertaining to the bombing mission and how it affected the lives of the citizens in his town.

We still communicate with some of the crew, mainly through Christmas cards.

For almost fifty years, the pilot, Lt. Ross, had nightmares about whether or not Hyman and Byrd had gotten the bailout order. Earl saw Hyman get hit. It's not known how Byrd, the tailgunner, died. Earl didn't see him come out of the tail section.

Sid Miller questioned whether Hyman and Byrd had been shot during battle, or after bail out. Germans showed Sid pictures of Sgts. Byrd and Hyman, and claimed their chutes didn't open. Miller called them liars.

"Hell, there wasn't a single wrinkle in the photographs!" Arthur Byrd and Arnold Hyman were buried at the crash site.

None of Lt. Ross' downed crew ever received the Distinguished Flying Cross medal, for valor presented in the face of the enemy.

The escape plan Earl helped devise at Stalag VII-A enabled many prisoners to make their ways to freedom. He hopes some of them, or their decendants are reading this account. He wishes he could recall the names of the men he escaped with. Who were Sonny and Mack? Who was Dave? Who was Casey with the split lip, and Gene, who died so tragically as he approached the bridge at Linz, Austria? Do they have families who wonder what happened back then...? Did Abie Schultz.... survive?

BIBLIOGRAPHY

Several sources provided material for this novel:

(1). "First Over Germany - A History Of The 306th Bombardment Group" by Russell A. Strong, 5323 Cheval Pl; Charlotte, NC. 28205. Printed by Hunter Printing Co., Winston-Salem, NC., revised edition 1990. Page 82, "Shot down over the Erla Works was Lt. Kelly Ross' 367th plane. Becoming prisoners with Ross were Lts. George Lewis and Sidney Miller, and Sgts. Earl Benson, William Hovekamp, Clyde Smith and Douglas Bowles. T/Sgt. Arnold E. Hyman and S/Sgt. Arthur Byrd, tail gunner and waist gunner, did not survive, etc."

(2). "A Chronicle Of Stalag XVII-B, Krems/Gneisendorf, Austria" by Luthor Victory, 600 E. Pearce St; Baytown, TX. 77520. Published by Corporate Sponsor, Marathon Oil Co. of Houston, TX. and JoAnn Salisbury of Crosby, TX., 1991. Page 174 of "Out Of The Turret And Into Hell": (Barracks chief named Tom Bagwell, etc. and Hovekamp in 35-A and Smith in barracks 37-A.) and page 198: (February 3, 1945, German records stated that there were 4,242 American Air Force prisoners in Stalag XVII-B.)

(3). Irving Berlin Music Company, 1633 Broadway, Suite 3801, New York, NY. 10019. Pgs. 171-172 include lyrics from "God Bless America." Used by permission.

(4). Information obtained from April 1986 issue of "306th Echoes" Vol. 11, No. 2, pages 4 - 7. Address: 2973 Heatherbrae Dr., Poland, OH. 44514

(5). Letters from USAF, (Ret'd.) Kelly G. Ross, 2820
      Kensington Rd, Redwood City, CA. 94061 (415) 366-6704.
      Insight for what happened 'up front' during fifth mission.

(6). Letters, in-person communication with navigator, Sid
      Miller, deceased Feb. 22, 1999, 400 Echo Rock Ct.,
      Roseville, CA. 95747 (916) 771-8581.

(7). In-person communication, extensive interviews with main
      character, Earl Benson, 1317 N. Matlock St., Mesa, AZ.
      85203-4324 (480) 827-8143

POST WAR NOTES

Five Benson brothers went to war, and all came home.
Howard drove for the Red Ball Express, delivering supplies to
the front, married Pearl, and they had two children. He passed
away in 1989.

Howard & Edward Benson - 1945

Edward (Red) fought in The Battle Of The Bulge, and suffered
frozen feet when his group was pinned down and forced to stand
in trenches of ice water. Red married Grace, and they had three
children. He passed away in 1987.

John, Jr. (Guy) was taken prisoner at Anzio. His guard failed to
take the rifle from John's shoulder. John dropped to one knee,
pulled the trigger, killed the guard, and escaped. He and first
wife had three sons, and divorced. Today, he and wife, Pat, and
grown children live in Massachussets. 'Jack-of-all-trades,'
good at most anything he sets out to do, he's an artist, who
studied in France after World War II.

Guy Bensen - August 1992

WWII Painting by Guy Bensen -1957

Ernest Benson - 1956

Ernest (Ernie) helped clear Normandy beaches, D-Day + 2, had two bulldozers blown from under him, and injured. He and wife Rachel had daughters. Ernie died in 1956.

Kenneth - Martha's Vinyard - 1943   Kenneth and Helen - Victory Garden - 1942

Kenneth married Helen. They had two daughters. One has his violin, the other his mandolin. He passed on in 1982. Helen lives in Connecticut.

Shirley married Peter, who had a daughter and a son. She passed away in 1974.

Edith married Andrew. They had three sons. She was an insurance investigator. She passed on in 1990.

Alice and Sam, had three children. She died in 1963.

Earl's parents divorced. John, Sr., ran the diner across from the bowling alley in Unionville. He died in 1947.
Hazel Benson remarried. She passed away in 1956.

Robert fought in the Korean Conflict. He and wife, Fran, live in Connecticut. They have two daughters and three grandsons.

Hazel Benson and youngest son, Robert (Bobby)

Earl and his father, John Henry Benson 1945

Bobby, Johnny (his artwork behind) and Earl Benson - August 1992

Earl Benson - 1945

Meeting the quadriplegics, Earl felt his injuries were insignificant. He turned down the Purple Heart. After prison camp, a psychiatrist asked what he wanted to do.

"I think I'll go fight the Japs." He reinlisted, went home, three months on leave, then to Lowry Field in Denver, Colorado for B-29 training. He saw Golden and Morrison, Colorado, and sent two beautiful postcards home.

He went to Boulder, Colorado to see Boulder Dam, didn't find it, but found Juanita, his wife of thirty-four years. Rose and Linda, daughters from her first marriage, were seven and four year olds. Later, Juanita and Earl lost twins, but in 1957, a daughter, with strawberry blond hair, was born.

Earl spent twenty years in the Air Force, eleven in Civil Service, drove city bus for Regional Transportation District in Boulder, and was a supervisor there when Juanita passed away in 1979. Rose Marie passed away, January, 2001. Remaining are two daughters, two grandsons, four granddaughters, three great-granddaughters, two great-great-grandsons, and.... hopefully many more, to pass his story on to.

Currently, three brothers survive, Earl, John and Robert.

Earl's been married to the author for over twenty years. They live in Mesa, Arizona. He was a Senior Vice-Commander in the East Valley Chapter of American Ex-Prisoners of War until diagnosed with colon cancer in 1995. (He's cancer-free now.) He lost sight in his left eye a few years ago. Cornea transplants saved vision in his right eye.

Vicky was Adjutant of the chapter and assisted a few ex-pows with filling out forms, helping qualify them for 100% disability. A few years ago, she pushed Earl to file a claim. He's now at 100%. The author has two sons, a daughter, four grandsons, and three granddaughters.

Sidney and Barbara Miller moved to Peoria, AZ. for a year, then moved back to northern California, an enjoyable reunion for the men, and the ladies became good friends, too. Vicky helped Sid get 100%, disability, and Sid's buddy letter helped Earl receive his Purple Heart award and medal.... fifty-three years late, but, worth the wait. Sid died, February 22, 1999.

V. Elaine Benson, born in Dearborn, Michigan, began her writing career with this novel. She earned a diploma from the Institute Of Children's Literature in 1998, and continues to improve her writing. Her goal: "Write well enough to enable a touching of the heart."

ISBN 1552128520

9 781552 128527